THE BEST OF
MARYA MANNES

The BEST of *MARYA MANNES*

Edited by

ROBERT MOTTLEY

RICHARDSON & STEIRMAN
NEW YORK
1986

I.S.B.N. 0-931933-13-7

L.C.C. 85-07297

Design by Deborah Daly
Typography by Dawn Typographic Services

The Best of Marya Mannes is published by Richardson & Steirman, Inc.
246 Fifth Avenue NYC, 10001

FOR MARYA

ACKNOWLEDGEMENTS

We are grateful for the assistance of Dr. Howard B. Gotlieb, Director of Special Collections, Mugar Memorial Library, Boston University, and to Charles Niles and Margaret Goostray on his staff; to the New York Society Library, and to the Mannes College and its president, Dr. Charles Kaufman.

We would like to thank, in particular, the following individuals for their help at various stages of this project: Julius and Deirdre Adler, Richard Beatty, Mary Beman, Eric Blau, Herbert E. Brown, Don Bruckner, Christopher Buckley, Jane Clancy, Christopher Clarkson, Joni Evans, Eleanor Friede, Robert N. Fishburn, Marion Gough, Peter P. Grey, Patricia Guinan, Dr. Frances Keene, Samantha King, Stephen Kimber, Allen T. Klots, the late Grace Knecht, William Koshland, Margaret McCampbell, Michael Mielziner, Pamela Mottley, Jacqueline Onassis, Mary Reed, Frances Russell, Elly Stone, Dorothy Uris, and Bretta Weiss.

Stewart Richardson

Robert Mottley

David Blow

A NOTE
FROM THE EDITOR

I have known Marya Mannes as a friend for eighteen years. On a number of occasions, we discussed what should go in and be left out of an anthology of her writing. Marya said repeatedly that she would drop topical references that might date a piece, change words to conform with current usage (such as black for Negro), and delete redundant paragraphs. She was adamant about not muting her opinions; I insisted that her underrated wartime reports from Spain and Portugal be reprinted intact. She wanted her poems in, and as broad a selection of topics as possible, even if that meant shortening articles.

When David Blow, Marya's son, asked me to compile and edit this collection, we knew that because of a debilitating illness in recent years, Marya could not help me. I accepted the assignment with an understanding that we would say up front that the anthology had been edited according to Marya's guidelines. I have done very little to my old friend's work, no more and probably less than she would have in her own hand, if that had been possible. Her words and spirit remain luminous.

Robert Mottley

New York City

TABLE OF CONTENTS

Table of Contents

Biographical Note

Marya Mannes was born in New York City on November 14, 1904. Her father, David Mannes (1866-1959), a native New Yorker and a professional violinist, conducted the New york Symphony from 1898 to 1912, and in 1916 founded the David Mannes School, now the Mannes College of Music. Her mother, Clara (1832-1948), daughter of the German maestro Leopold DAmrosch (1832-1885), married David Mannes in 1898. A pianist, Clara Mannes accompanied Pablo Casals, performed with the Kneisel Quartet, and toured professionally with her husband.

Marya Mannes's brother, Leopold (1899-1964), was a composer, a concert pianist and an inventive chemist. He collaborated with Leopold godowsky, another musician-scientist, to create the first integral tripack color film in 1935, marketed by the Eastman Kodak Co. as Kodachrome. Her uncle, Walter Damrosch (1862-1950), founded the Damrosch Opera Company in New York, active from 1894 to 1899, and conducted symphonic concerts with the New York Philharmonic (1902-3) and Symphony Orchestra, as the early Philharmonic was called after reorganization, from 1903 to 1926.

Marya graduated from the Veltin School for Girls in New York City, where she was known as Marie or "Ma Mie," in 1923. She was married (and divorced) three times: in 1926 to Jo Mielziner, later to become a famous theatrical set designer; in 1937 to Richard Blow, an artist, and in 1948 to Christopher Clarkson, a diplomat.

Marya Mannes began her professional writing career as an associate editor for *Vogue* in 1933, and was feature editor when she resigned in 1936. She served abroad as an intelligence analyst for the U.S. government from 1942 to 1945, and free-lanced in earnest after the war. In time, her by-line would appear on 329 articles, 275 of them written for Max Ascoli, editor of *The Reporter*, on which she worked as a staff writer from 1952 to 1963. Beginning in 1958, Marya appeared numerous times on network television, in the roles of critic, arbiter, social commentator, and (her favorite) Cassandra of the media. In 1960, she began to lecture around the country.

Her published nonfiction includes three collections of essays,

More in Anger (1958), *The New York I Know* (1961), and *But Will It Sell?* (1964); an autobiography, *Out Of My Time* (1971), and *Last Rights* (1973). Her first novel, *Message from a Stranger* (1948), had an extended market life in hardbound and paperback editions. A second novel, *They* (1968), made a particularly strong impact as a teleplay filmed with Cornelia Otis Skinner.

Marya's terse poems, often mocking and fatal for their targets, were frequently spurred by news vignettes that caught her eye. Her final drafts and much unpublished material, including five novels, 16 plays, 19 short stories, sketches for numerous essays and speeches, and many "pensees" scrawled in margins, have been given to Boston University.

Marya lives today in the San Francisco area near her only son, David Blow.

THE BEST OF
MARYA MANNES

Part I

As a
Reporter

FLORENCE, 1938

That summer of 1938, Hitler and Mussolini met in Florence. On the day this was to happen, most prudent citizens stayed home and all known dissidents were cleared from sensitive areas.

I walked alone down the long hill to Florence, impelled to see what I hated and dreaded most.

The route of the dictators' passage was not made public. The streets were therefore unusually empty for that mecca of tourists and, in fact, for any Italian city. Little clumps of people stood at several intersections and along the Arno, but their silence was strange and unusual. As I wandered around the streets I heard only one noise, repeated at intervals. It came from loudspeakers attached to the cornices of buildings. From a crackling, highly amplified soundtrack they roared "Duce! Duce! Duce!" as from the mouths of watching masses.

After almost an hour of this, bored, I retraced my steps to the Ponte di Ferro, and finding an air of expectancy in the group clustered there by the river, decided to join them.

In no more than ten minutes, with no warning, they drove along the Lungarno toward us in an open car: Hitler and Mussolini side by side. As they turned slowly toward the Ponte di Ferro, they were no more than twelve feet away. In that frozen minute, I noticed two things. Hitler's moustache and hair were rusty, not black as the pictures showed them.

And, next to him, Mussolini looked like a human being. Several people raised their arms and cried "Duce! Duce!" but the rest seemed dazed.

I was, myself. All I could think of all the way up the hill to Piazza Calda was that I could have thrown some flowers and a bomb into that car with ease. And that I would have happily died for having done so.

3

LETTER
FROM LISBON
(JUNE 25, 1944)

So far, the repercussions of the Allied landings in France have been slight in this capital. On D-Day, the British-American colony here held a service at the Church of the Estrela. A group of Portuguese stood in the brilliant sun to watch them go in, the diplomatic staffs of both nations consciously grave, the military and naval representatives in the uniforms they may wear only on state occasions. Members of the Chinese and Brazilian legations and representatives of the Free French office here joined the Americans and British in prayer; so did members of the Dutch, Polish, Greek, Norwegian, and Belgian missions. The service was Anglican and brief. In the course of the day, papers were sold out edition after edition, one newsboy being mobbed in the square of the Rocio, and there were a few individual expressions of joy at the news from pro-Ally Portuguese. However, faces of most Portuguese were noncommital, although you heard the word "invasion" wherever you went. The Portuguese hold fast to their neutrality, which is one of emotion as well as of national policy. There had been a more noticeable reaction to the suspension of wolfram shipments to Germany, worry that reprisals might be the price. All the windows in Lisbon are still taped because of earlier worries. If the Germans here were moved by the D-Day news, they didn't show it. They continued to eat, to smile, to appear in their usual haunts. Whether they are ordered to maintain a cheerful front, or are actually not alarmed, or are merely happy to be in a position of comparative, if temporary safety, it is hard to say. Whatever is the case, they have better face than their Japanese allies, several of whom, on the night of the invasion, were wandering about the Casino at Estoril looking more forlorn than inscrutable. The Japs keep to themselves, apparently because they are not welcome anywhere, even among their tolerant hosts.

However familiar the concept of neutrality may be, the practice of it is constantly surprising to the visiting belligerent. Two members of the German embassy sit next to you in a restaurant; you look at them, they look at you, but they do not exist as fellow human beings. You have the sensation that there is a pilotfilm partition between you and them. They are an exhibit marked "enemy. Do not touch." There are Nazi posters on many shop fronts and walls. On the newsstands, which seem as profuse and cluttered as our own, *Signal,* an opulent German illustrated monthly, is stacked next to *Collier's, Time, Life,* and the O.W.I. [Office of War Information]'s magazine *Victory.* The English *Vogue* is next to the Portuguese *Voga. The Daily Telegraph,* the *Volkischer Beobachter,* the *Journal de Genève, Paris-Soir,* all are there. *Victory* and other O.W.I. publications are bought up as they arrive here. Free copies are supplied to hairdressers and hotels, but they disappear by the end of the first day.

The German propaganda line concentrates largely on the "terror bombings" of the Anglo-American "gangster pilots." This has not been without effect on the neutrals, many of whom are openly deploring American bombing because they feel that since nobody attacked our country (with the exception of Pearl Harbor), we have no right to lay waste to Europe. This attitude, possibly hard to reconcile with the ultrarealistic basis of neutrality, is worth watching. The airwaves, of course, are free to all. Anyone who has listened to the shortwave at home knows the sardonic and rather godlike amusement to be derived from tuning from Vichy to Berlin to the BBC. Here this sort of amusement is easier to come by. On one local radio station there will be a Gershwin record, followed by a German close-harmony crooning of American cowboy songs, followed in turn by the Russian "Song of the Plains." In view of the strong anti-Soviet feeling here, it's always possible that the last number may have been a slip. Of all news broadcasts, those of the BBC still lead the field in clarity of reception and credibility. Vichy is sometimes surprisingly informative. Shortwave from America is hard to get, and as yet few people seem to listen to our London broadcasts.

The material rewards of neutrality are apparent enough. The men of Portugal are alive and at home, and living is very comfortable for those who have money. Prices have gone up about 50 percent in the last two years, but there are plenty of people who can afford to pay them. There are also plenty who cannot. The shops in Lisbon are dazzling. You can buy anything from nylons to rubber bathing caps, from Parker pens to Pep. The nylons come from France, are as good as ours, and cost about $5.00. Swiss watches flood the market, and there are armies of tin soldiers. The windows glitter with the traditional Portuguese gold-filigree jewelry. There is an endless choice of beautiful French silks, if you can afford $15.00 and more a yard for them. Or you can get a real Piguet or Lelong model from Paris, starting at about $110 for a day dress that has the typical French excellence of detail. As for local fashions, the heads and feet of the Portuguese women are notable: the hats, Paris-inspired, are towering confections of straw, heavily loaded with ribbon, veiling, or flowers, the crown usually looking like an inverted basket; the shoes have high cork-wedge soles, very practical for the cobbled ramps of Lisbon. For the women who carry utilitarian baskets on their heads, bare feet are even more practical. Liquor is plentiful. Good Scotch comes to about $5.50 a quart; the best English gin, which is growing scarce, costs almost as much. Most people drink the local gin. There is one excellent brand manufactured here by an Englishman named Phazey. The Portuguese wines have strength and character. Rationing exists, but the foreigner is almost unaware of it. There is, however, a shortage of sugar, and the bread is gray, damp, and scarce. Desserts consist of fruit, which abounds, and cheese, which is very good. There is an enormous variety of fresh fish and no lack of meat.

In general, the hotels are modern and immaculate. On the whole, the Portuguese are a clean and tidy people, thoughtful about the comfort of others. In Lisbon proper, the great luxury hotel is the Aviz. It has only thirty-odd rooms, costs upwards of fifteen dollars a day (with meals), and seems to be made of solid-gold filigree. High-ranking diplomats and international financiers stay there, as do other people of means who merely want to live as well as they can. The Avenida Palace and the Tivoli are both E. Phillips Oppenheim products, patronized by agents of both camps, while the Francfort is more exclusively a German hangout. Since by this time nearly everyone knows who everyone else is, and what he is up to, the spy business is less menacing than humorous. There are doubtless plenty of machinations still afoot, but the urgency is gone. Friend and foe here are aware that the real doings are on the battlefronts, and that Lisbon is, for the moment, chiefly a rumor bed and a sounding board, strangely remote in spite of its nearness to war. The suspicion exists, however, that Portugal may become the chief exit for the drowning rats, and some interesting and possibly important faces may be passing through. Sweden is too near Russia, and Switzerland is a trap. As long as the peninsula is not isolated entirely, Portugal is the reasonable alternative.

Lisbon is hilly, hot, noisy, and confusing. It is also beautiful, since every height gives a view of the harbor and the avenues are decorated by palms, flowering jacarandas, or brilliant flower beds. The worst traffic congestion is on Friday, Saturday, and Monday, when private cars are allowed on the streets. On other days traffic is confined to taxis and to diplomatic and other cars with special privileges. Whatever their status, all motorists drive wildly and blow their horns every three seconds. The fortunate, to escape the cacophony and heat, live in Estoril and commute by electric railway or car. Estoril, which is at the mouth of the Tagus, twenty miles due west of Lisbon, has a typical Mediterranean resort quality: esplanade palms, cabanas, big white hotels, floral patches of magenta and vermilion, expensive small shops, and, commanding all this from a height, the Casino. The stringent beach rules are less Mediterranean. Men must wear trunks and tops; women must wear tops and skirts. Women have been fined five hundred escudos for dropping their shoulder straps. All this has been explained as a reaction to the refugee invasion of 1940, with its supposed exhibitionism. Whatever the reason, it is one of the local gripes among foreigners. The gambling rooms at the Casino are oddly depressing. The overhead lighting is bleak, people do not dress, and there is nothing festive in the air. There is not even the feverish greed of the jewel-encrusted old ladies one used to see in prewar casinos. The Germans are there, but only the "smaller" ones. You get the feeling that the big ones don't bother.

The absence of refugees here is very noticeable. Those who have never received their exit visas are still confined to a refugee area in the Caldas de Painha, seventy miles northwest of Lisbon, and will probably stay there indefinitely, either from choice or apathy. All the rest have left the country. The hotels in Estoril, however, still harbor some notable exiles from time to time. Dino Grandi has been here, and so have Juan March, Franco's financier, now in his disfavor, and Alba, Spanish foreign minister under Alfonso. The romantic essence of Portugal, though, is not in the exiles or the diplomatic staffs, it is the actual country, which is far more beautiful than most people know, because it has been far less advertised than other places. The wild beaches of Guincho, the headlands of Cabo da Roca (the Calais of the Atlantic Channel), the steep and ancient hills of Cintra, the old gray palaces smothered in leaves, all this has the pattern of a dream, and blowing through everything continuously is the wind of the open Atlantic, which has an edge and vigor that no Mediterranean wind has.

The Portuguese bullfight is an exciting show, far less bloody and turgid than the Spanish kind. For one thing, the native bull-fighter is on horseback; for another, the bull is not killed; finally, his horns are blunted and wrapped so that he cannot gore. The Portuguese fighter in the last important *corrida,* held at the Campo Pequeno, was Joao Branco Nuncio, elegant in an eighteenth-century black satin suit and tricorne embroidered with silver. His tasseled horse was equally elegant, with precise, delicate legs and a fine arch to his neck. Nuncio would attract the bull's attention, horse and bull would gallop at each other, Nuncio would plant his dart on the bull's neck, horse and man would sideswipe the horns and trot away. In planting the dart, Nuncio would drop the reins and control the horse with his knees. (Nuncio, by the way, is reported to have been a huge success in Spain, where the crowd at the last *corrida* yelled, "You are no Nuncio, you are the Pope!") On the program with Nuncio in Lisbon this time were the magnificent *espada* Manolete, who is Spanish, and the Mexican Arruza, young, handsome, and very brave, but not as polished as Manolete. Both Manolete and Arruza fought on foot, after a group of local toreadors had got the bull irritated enough to charge. Manolete was in salmon pink and silver-crusted yellow, with a turquoise tie. Arruza was in bottle green and silver. Manolete brought the house down with the sensational ease of his *"veronicas."* Arruza triumphed when he faced the bull, arms outstretched, moving the cape from side to side behind him. The bull charged, first to one side, then to the other, Arruza's body being exposed the entire time. For this the horns were unsheathed. Both fighters substituted a final dart for the Spanish sword, planting it in the traditional part of the neck. When they were through, the women threw flowers and the men threw hats into the ring. The bullfighters kept the flowers and hurled back the hats.

The crowds at the bullfight looked like citizens of a happy country. Portugal has prospered in these war years. There are new buildings everywhere, new roads are in the making, and the trains run on time. If the fishwives have gaunt cheeks, the beauty of their walk under their headbaskets piled with fish or fruit may testify to some fundamental inner order. Being poor, they have suffered, and they possess at least a dignity of feature here not apparent elsewhere. Easy living and an absence of strong feeling are not becoming to the human psyche, and there is a price, however imponderable, for remaining at peace. If you hate no one, the chances are that you love no one; and in this case, two negatives do not make an affirmative.

LETTER
FROM MADRID
(SEPTEMBER 15, 1944)

There was no dancing in the streets of Madrid to celebrate the liberation of Paris. If the members of the battered left did any rejoicing, they wisely did it behind closed doors. The right, aware that this liberation meant the loosening of forces that might threaten the Spanish state, had nothing much to rejoice over. Later, when the Allies landed on the southern coast of France, General Franco ordered thirty thousand troops to the eastern frontier, just in case any enthusiastic French Maquis or vengeful Spanish Republicans happened to spill over the border. These troops had nothing much to do beyond escorting several hundred German customs guards and garrison troops, who had jumped quickly across the frontier to an interment camp where they were made comfortable. Later still, when the Allied armies were beginning their march into Germany, Franco was off in the northern provinces dispensing medals, the Foreign Minister was in San Sebastian, and most other responsible members of the government were vacationing on the Catalan or Basque beaches. Madrid, the capital, was for all practical diplomatic purposes, a deserted city. This nice demonstration of apathy was typical of the General, who recently referred to the Second World War as a conflict between "village nationalisms."

The Germans in Madrid seemed to accept their isolation from the Fatherland with equanimity. Some of them gave the impression of being distinctly relieved at having been provided by the enemy with excellent alibis for sitting out the disaster that is impending at home. They would no longer even be able to send back reports. One German agent was overheard saying, "Thank God the paper war is over." The end of Vichy France brought the de Gaullist French mission here into public life and closed up the officially recognized Vichy embassy. The de Gaullist group, headed by M. Truelle, a suave career diplomat, and animated by an extraordinary priest named Boyer-Mas, had operated in a dusty palace lent them by a sympathetic Spanish duchess. The atmosphere of the mission had, before the liberation, been forlorn and slightly wistful. Truelle had said to a friend, "I would like to be made an honest woman." He was. Overnight the building was given a noticeable sprucing-up, the number of clerks multiplied, and appointment slips were brought out for callers to sign before they could confer with members of the staff.

The doors of the embassies and legations in Madrid are guarded by Spanish militiamen. At the Allied missions, these men sprawl on chairs, usually half-asleep, their guns hanging from their shoulders. They do not rise, even for ambassadors, and in fact seldom bother to look up when someone enters or leaves. At the German embassy, they snap to attention and raise their right arm in the Fascist salute when officials appear. Madrid is still the most Prussian place in Spain. It is by no means Berlin, however. The Nazi pattern in Berlin came from the people themselves; the Fascist pattern in Madrid has been imposed from without. The Spaniard is essentially a nonconformist. He conforms only under great pressure, and at the moment he does so because of his profound fear of another civil war. Those Spaniards afflicted with the Fascist virus are a minority. That minority, however, is armed.

Franco is the generalissimo of this band, but the spiritual leader is the late José Antonio Primo de Rivera, eldest son of the former dictator. Franco is the object of more and more criticism from the majority of his countrymen, who seem weary of his vanity, his lush rhetoric, and his apparent ignorance of the serious issues that Spain should be, but is not, facing. José Antonio, being dead, is not losing favor. His photographs, which are displayed beside Franco's everywhere, show that he was a handsome young man who wore an open-necked white shirt and had the baffling, liquid stare expected of a visionary and a mystic. He started the youth movement that flowered into the Falange, the Spanish equivalent of the National Socialist Party. He was an idealistic, not very intelligent man, and he appears to have believed with great sincerity in the vision of a new and revitalized Spain that could be achieved with a handful of inspirational slogans and a few simple physical exercises. he was executed by the Loyalists during the Civil War and thus became, in the eyes of his followers, a martyr. He is buried, a few steps from the crucifix on the high altar and not far from several Spanish kings, in the church of the Escorial, and his slogans, full of references to work and sacrifice and to the blood-brotherhood of the Falange, appear on the walls of government buildings and in the mastheads of the newspapers. this idolatry shocks not only many foreigners but many Spaniards as well. Equally shocking, at least to American visitors, is the manner in which the aristocracy of Madrid evades the twentieth century. The aristocrats live much as their ancestors lived a hundred years ago, idle, superior, intently oblivious of anyone but themselves. Their fear of Communism is pathological. Their family life, so glorified in Fascist dogma, takes the form of an endless series of cocktail parties, dinners, infidelities, and fittings. Madrid makes one think at times not only of Nazi Berlin but of Versailles before the French Revolution. You cannot, of course, speak of these things here. You cannot speak of the prison under the Seguridad Building, in the Puerta del sol, Madrid's Times Square, in which political suspects are confined to cells below ground, where the roar of the traffic overhead is so loud that conversation is impossible. You cannot speak, either, of the thousands of *rojos* (Reds) who are hiding in the hills of the northern provinces.

At first glance, the capital of Spain has a calm and prosperous look. The city, built on a high plateau, is spacious and attractive, with fine, broad avenues shaded by big trees. The town is full of pretty young girls walking in twos and threes, their hair in long bobs, their legs bare, their handbags slung over their shoulders. They dress in skirts and blouses and wear four-inch heels because they are so short. In the summer most of the men wear white coats, gray trousers, and black glasses, which makes them all look alike. There are few beggars. The crowds are orderly; people cross the streets only where the signs tell them to. The food in the restaurants is plentiful. You can have every variety of meat and fish. The only shortage is bread.

These first impressions make you receptive to the talk of government spokesmen who try hard, with statistics, to show you that Spain has prospered under Franco. It is difficult not to feel that the liberal newspapers and magazines in England and the United States may be mistaken about the economic condition of Spain. Then you begin to notice things, and hear things. You learn that the brilliantly uniformed army officers who stride down the avenues have to make money on the side to live up to their station. Many of them operate little businesses, usually on the black market. You find that the enlisted men, in their crumpled khaki, earn twenty-five centavos a day (around two cents), which happens to be the Madrid streetcar fare. The ceiling on a laborer's wages is fifteen pesetas, or a dollar thirty-five, a day.

The Ritz in Madrid is one of the few great luxury hotels still operating in Europe. It is managed by a Belgian family of distinctly German orientation; the members of this family, attired always in funeral black and seldom speaking above a whisper, are conspicuously rude in a profession famous for its arrogance, and in spite of the elegance of the rooms and the impeccable service, the atmosphere of the place is, to an American, uncomfortable and hostile. The Ritz is part of Madrid's facade. At the other extreme are the queues, blocks long, of ragged people waiting outside the British Press and O.W.I. offices for news of the war. When you ask who they are, some people will tell you that they are the porters and messengers of business houses waiting for the mimeographed Allied news releases to take back to their employers. Others will shrug and say, "They're only *rojos.*" Whatever they are, they snatch the bulletins with almost frightening avidity, stand around on the street reading them, then stuff them in their pockets and shuffle away.

There is enthusiasm for the Allies among the workers in Madrid. Their faces brighten when they learn that you are British or American, and they shake your hand warmly. There is some enthusiasm among the employers, but you get the impression that they are for us only because we are winning now. There have always been a few Anglophiles among the rich and aristocratic, but most well-to-do Spaniards were until recently either indifferent to the war or impressed by the Germans. Now these people appear to be impressed reluctantly by us. British and American war news is finally being given generous space in the Spanish papers, particularly in two called *Ya* and *ABC*. Relatively little space is given in these two papers to German and Russian communiqués; the grudging respect the Spanish Right has for the Allies does not include the Soviet Union. The government has stopped jamming the BBC Spanish-language programs. (The best music on the air, most Spaniards feel, is still being broadcast from Berlin.) Censorship continues to exclude all American magazines and books. American movies are shown, but the censorship imposed by the Church causes most of the films to be cut heavily, which often distorts the story drastically. The Madrid exhibitors of *Wuthering Heights,* for example, were required to delete the scene in which Cathy dies in Heathcliff's arms. The Church considered the situation adulterous because the two were not husband and wife. In another film, two lovers were transformed by the Spanish subtitles into brother and sister, because they were shown on several occasions alone together in a room.

The Spanish aristocrats continue to regard Germany as a Christian and civilized country and a bulwark against Communism. They think America is powerful and they like our products, but they do not consider us either very Christian or very cultured. This is particularly the fault of our propaganda, which concerns itself almost entirely with military might, whereas the Germans, until recent events made it difficult, shipped in publications full of articles on art, music, and philosophy. The Spaniards in power respect the British, but they cannot forget the British intervention in their Civil War. Americans are accepted as victors but are not wanted as friends.

The Germans have been here so long and have handled their propaganda so skillfully that even their total defeat will not break their hold on Spain immediately. Their influence goes deep, economically and culturally. You can see their mark everywhere, in the shape of the Spanish Army helmet, in the German marching songs that are sung to Spanish words by the Falangist youths, and in the outstretched-arm salute. The police still work in close cooperation with the Gestapo. Every hotel room is searched regularly and thoroughly. Picked hotel employees, equipped with skeleton keys that will open any luggage, assist the police in their work, and telephones are tapped.

But what some misguided porter does for the Gestapo in a hotel room is a trivial thing. The important, the serious thing is that Madrid under the Falange is not Spain. Part of Spain is in the Prado: in El Greco, Velásquez, Goya. The rest is in ambush, waiting.

LETTER
FROM
BARCELONA
(OCTOBER 1, 1944)

Barcelona is a long, long way from Madrid. Barcelona is Catalan and Madrid is Castilian, and the mountains that separate Catalonia from France are not as high as the invisible barrier between Catalonia and Castile. Madrid is the past and Barcelona the future of a once-great nation. Like all seaports, Barcelona is a natural city, which has grown out of its geography. Madrid is an artificial city, an arbitrary capital.

The long, wide, leafy boulevards of Barcelona, the Ramblas, the Paseo de Gracia, the Diagonal, give the city a bright, aerated quality that Madrid lacks. The people jaywalk and no whistle jerks them back. You see fewer army officers, fewer police, and little evidence of the pervasive and almost Prussian bureaucracy of the capital. In the morning, the streets are crowded with people on their way to work, for nearly everyone works here. People work in Madrid, too, but there two hours in an office is considered a tough day for a man, and no nice woman works at all. The Barcelona girls are not as pretty as the Madrilenians, but they walk with freedom and assurance, almost like American girls. Barcelona has, in general, an American spirit; its energy, eagerness, curiosity, and humor provide a contrast to the dark, ingrowing nationalism of central Spain. The Catalan is by temperament a progressive. He has plenty of traditions, but he is receptive to new ideas. The industrialists of Catalonia are, of course, conservative, but even they are receptive to change and friendly to America. Catalan intellectuals, artists, and workers, muzzled and frustrated though they are at the moment, are more than receptive and more than friendly. They are only a hundred miles from a free France, and from their exiled and resur-

16

gent countrymen there.

The Catalan has some special vitality as the result of the fact that he produces, not only for himself, but for most of Spain. Catalonia provides silk, cotton goods, olive oil, and wine. It is also the peninsula's breeding ground for talent. The mysticism of Montserrat and the Mediterranean lightness of spirit make a fine creative mold. The combination is nowhere more visible than in the Barcelona Cathedral. Inside it is dim and grandiose, but in the courtyard there are fountains, geese, magnolias, and children playing. Catalonia has produced many of the best modern Spanish painters, beginning with Ruisnol and Fortuny, in the late nineteenth century, and continuing with Dali. Madrid has only one gallery which exhibits contemporary art; Barcelona has thirty. The Catalonian taste is evident everywhere, in the city's shop windows, which are among the most elegant in the world, in its clothes, in its ceramics. The Barcelona Opera, which ranks with the Paris Opera and La Scala, has been having some brilliant seasons, owing partly to the contributions of the best German singers and musicians. It is also offering a novelty, a Japanese conductor, well thought of here, who is frequently seen at the Ritz with a copy of the London *Daily Mail* under his arm. The old Ballet Russe always included Barcelona in its tours. The Catalans themselves do a great deal of ritualistic, complicated street dancing. Pablo Casals, probably the world's greatest cellist, is a Catalan.

The Catalans read a lot, but they are now officially restricted, for the most part, to historical romances (there is safety only in the past) and to government-inspired essays. One of the most popular books at present, and one that the government has not plugged, is a biography of Churchill; another is a volume of Mickey Mouse comic strips in Spanish. There are only a few French books and almost no English or American ones. The newspapers, except for the weekly *Destino*, which has somehow managed to be pro-Ally all along, are uniform and without substance. Most of their space is devoted to Falange activities, to the Church, and to the enthusiastic receptions

El Caudillo is presumably receiving throughout Spain. They are also given to the discursive, emotional journalism in which every piece begins with a series of rhetorical questions. The only publication which contains the characteristically caustic and crazy Spanish humor is *Codorniz,* a completely nonpolitical weekly that devotes itself to gags, jokes, satires, and expert cartoons.

Barcelona is full of places to go at night, from large outdoor restaurants with good dance bands to small joints in the narrow streets of the Barriocinos, where Andalusian entertainers sing flamenco until five in the morning. The Catalans love flamenco, which has the hopped-up, frenetic quality of a jam session, but with profoundly tragic undertones. The city also has a lot of pleasantly bohemian cafés where amateurs get up and sing or dance before quiet, shabby audiences. Besides all this, there are beautiful beaches an hour away, and nearby there are mountain villages, with rapid streams and cool, dry air, as a summer antidote to the smothering humidity of the city.

Because of all of its physical and spirtual wealth, Catalonia is resented by the other, poorer regions of Spain. In the interest of Falange unity, the Madrid government has attempted to level out the people of Spain. This leveling has been done not by law but by a series of restrictive measures that amount to the same thing. The Catalan language may not be printed, sung, or spoken in public. Taxes are theoretically the same for all of Spain, but their collection is enforced rigidly only in Catalonia. There is no law against establishing new businesses in Catalonia, but innumerable bureaucratic obstacles are put in a Catalan manufacturer's way, and "inspectors" are sent out from Madrid to supervise Catalan industry. These men receive no salary; instead, they are given 40 percent of any fines collected for infractions, however trivial, of government regulations. Needless to say, they live in affluence if not in the hearts of their countrymen.

There is a certain amount of separatist talk from time to time, as there always has been, but few intelligent Catalans seem to want an independent state. They merely want, and think they deserve, certain personal and cultural liberties which are now withheld. Catalans in industrial and financial circles believe that these and other aims will be realized before long, probably, as they might be expected to think, through the establishment of a constitutional monarchy. Photographs of Juan II (now in Switzerland) hang in many offices, and copies of his plan for a new government are circulated discreetly. This business group is violently opposed to Franco and Falangism, but it feels that Spaniards are not yet capable of sustaining a real democracy. Some Catalan priests are also members of this conservative opposition to the Fascist regime. The majority of the workers, who have a long record of revolutionary action, are not content to place their hopes in Juan II. But whatever happens, Barcelona is united in its hatred of Falangist control, and Catalans of all groups will be in the first wave of revolt.

Most Catalans were elated over the change of neighbors across the border in August. They and the Basques, of all the Spaniards, have been the least affected by German propaganda. However, Catalonia is still full of Germans, most of whom came here to engage in both business and intelligence. Until recently, Lufthansa was operating a regular Berlin-Stuttgart-Barcelona air service, and there was a constant coming and going of Nazi agents. Now that German planes can no longer stop off at Lyon and are in danger of being shot down by Allied fighters anyway, this traffic has just about ceased, and a regiment of spies is immobilized. No one knows what will happen to them. Some have already changed their names and moved to smaller towns. Some have left for South America. Most of those remaining are concentrating on their legitimate businesses. Intelligence can wait.

The Nazis are subjected, along with other visitors, to an unusual torture devised by Catalan elevator boys. When taking passengers up or down, the operator faces them, instead of toward the door, and keeps his eye steadily on them. The elevator is very small, the trip very slow, and the silence very heavy. There is no telling what this experience may do to the conscience of a retired spy.

LETTER
FROM
JERUSALEM
(AUGUST 4, 1946)

At three o'clock in the afternoon last Friday, the people of Tel Aviv milled out into the hot streets from their homes, after four days of an all-but-total curfew; a curfew that had been imposed, following the death in a Jerusalem hospital of the ninety-first victim of the bombing of the King David Hotel, because it was believed that somewhere in their midst the men responsible for this latest development in a tragically muddled situation were hidden. A search of Tel Aviv had then been conducted as a full-scale military operation. Men here who went through the fighting in Europe are inclined to regard Major General A. J. H. Cassels's isolation and search of Tel Aviv, a Jewish city of almost two hundred thousand, as a military act of almost unparalleled precision, completeness, and discipline.

On the second day of the search, another American and I left Jerusalem for Tel Aviv in a car with a Jewish chauffeur, both supplied by the Jewish Agency, the official Zionist organization in Palestine. We already had passes, issued by the British Public Information officer, which allowed us to circulate in Jerusalem after the six-o' clock curfew there and to move about in most parts of Palestine, but they were no good where we were going, so our first objective en route was the Army's headquarters in Jaffa, at which we asked permission to enter Tel Aviv. Jaffa, an hour's drive from Jerusalem, is Tel Aviv's Arab neighbor. Headquarters was in the large, modern Curtis Building, which was surrounded, as are all public buildings in Palestine, by a thicket of barbed wire. Posted around it was a guard of Arab officers of the Palestine police, stalwart and saturnine men in black astrakan caps. The offices of the lieutenant colonel who signed and gave us our passes to enter Tel Aviv seemed to be in the center from which the search of the troubled city was being directed. Large, detailed maps of Tel Aviv were hung on the walls, a radio operator sat with earphones clamped over his head, young officers tensely studied papers at their desks, and there was a steady buzz of messages and orders, and an atmosphere of efficiency and tension. We had just thanked the colonel and were about to leave when General Cassels walked in. He is tall and urbane, with a long, sallow perceptive face that is not at all in the British military tradition. This thirty-nine-year-old general, wearing the red beret of the Sixth Airborne Division on his head and its red tabs on his socks, and carrying a swagger stick under his arm, was in charge of the Tel Aviv operation. If the problems and implications of the situation worried him, he showed no sign of it. "Go where you like," he said. "Those passes will get you into the city."

The passes did get us in, but only after they had been examined by a large number of guards. Every road into Tel Aviv was closed by a barrier of barbed wire, tanks, troops of the airborne division, and police. Behind the barriers was a city seemingly devoid of civilian life. The streets lay white and, for the most part, deserted in the sun. The shutters of the flat, modern houses were closed and their balconies were empty. No Jew, and that meant no resident, was visible or audible. Occasionally, a light tank or a Bren-gun carrier clattered through the streets. At every intersection, airborne soldiers in red berets stopped us and demanded our passes and that of our driver. Some glanced quickly at our credentials and let us through; others questioned even the passes the army had given us in Jaffa. "Anyone could forge those," said a young British corporal contemptuously. "But they are signed by your colonel," I said, pointing to the signature. "Never 'eard of him," the soldier said. "These bloody colonels change every day." But he waved us on.

After asking directions of five or six guards, we came to a point where the search for terrorists was in progress, a section of a residential district in which a concentration of lorries, armored cars, jeeps, troops, and police had drawn up before a group of small white apartment buildings. Groups of soldiers and police were entering the houses, some to search the premises and others to lead out every occupant they found. The balconies were crowded with people who, we discovered, had not been examined and, while waiting their turn, were watching what was happening to those the authorities had already taken out of the buildings. Most of the men wore shorts and open shirts, conventional Coney Island attire. Many of the young women were handsome in a plump way, and the children seemed above average in sturdiness. The screening of these people took place right there, at a long table that had been set up in the shade of some trees in front of one of the houses. Behind the table sat several British members of the Palestine police, and before them filed the people from the apartments, showing their documents and answering questions. Mothers and children were in most cases sent back to their homes immediately. Many of the men and a few single women were loaded into lorries and taken away for further screening.

We watched several similar search operations and saw nothing in the nature of violence. The soldiers, in spite of the now-notorious order of General Evelyn Hugh Barker, commander of the British forces in Palestine, to make the Jews "aware of the contempt and loathing with which we regard their conduct," behaved quietly and resorted to a minimum of physical persuasion. The people of Tel Aviv were passive and obedient, and many took the search with a sardonic good humor. The groups on the balconies chatted in Hebrew and German and smiled and waved at those who went off in the lorries, and they waved back, grimacing or smiling. A few children whimpered, but it might have been just the heat, or improper feeding caused by the fact that until the end of the second day of the curfew, when it was decided to let the people out to shop between five and seven, they had no fresh food. A few old men with black beards and black skullcaps gazed mournfully at the proceedings, but of desperation or even of acute resentment there was no sign. Only the British Palestine police, in their black-visored caps, looked harassed and strained, as if aware of the tensions about them and of their own uneasy relation to these people.

We followed one of the lorries to brigade headquarters, set up in a boys' school, where the men and single women who had not been released after their first screening were given a second, more thorough going over. Most of the building was being used to billet airborne troops, but the courtyard and one small wing had been turned into a temporary detention center. The lieutenant colonel in charge of the second screening was natty and unruffled. Twirling his swagger stick and followed by a battered, panting, bowlegged boxer, he led us on a tour of inspection. The courtyard was filled with people, mostly men, a large proportion of whom were unkempt and disheveled. The colonel proceeded to describe, with wry distaste, the disreputable appearance of the majority of the people who had been screened under his supervision during the past few months. Then he issued an order to some subordinates, who in good airborne style, all but snapped their arms off saluting. "Get the poor devils home, for God's sake," he said. "And speed it up."

He led us back into headquarters and went into a room in which a number of officers were sitting at a row of tables checking through piles of documents. As we hesitated in the doorway, he beckoned to us; we entered and saw, standing opposite the officers, with his back to a bare white wall, a small man with a thick black beard and felt hat. Facing him was a soldier holding a rifle with bayonet fixed; two other soldiers, also with bayonets fixed, flanked him. No one spoke. The officers continued to check their documents. The man stood there. Presently he turned his head slowly and looked at us, and in his eyes was a terrible, black, burning mixture of fanaticism, hatred, and defiance. "Nasty bit of work, that," said the colonel. "We have good reason to believe he's one of the leading members of the Stern gang." We asked him what the three soldiers with bayonets were doing. "We're waiting for him to talk," said the colonel, and led us out of the room. I asked the colonel whether the search of Tel Aviv would be worth all the trouble it involved and the conflicting emotions it had aroused. "Every bit of it," he replied. "We're getting a pile of stuff. There's no doubt that the terrorists had their stores and headquarters here. It's tough on the innocent, but we couldn't get the goods on the rest in any other way."

Figures that have been compiled on the Tel Aviv search reveal that, in all, 102,000 people were screened (the aged, sick, and extremely young were passed by) and that 748 men were sent to a detention camp at Rafa for further examination and 20 women to one at Latrun. In answer to questions about the need for such drastic measures, General Cassels has said that the only alternative would have been for the people of Tel Aviv to come forward and offer assistance. Neither the people of Tel Aviv nor any of the Jews elsewhere in Palestine did come forward to offer assistance. Their talk is heavy with bitterness and apprehension. They can see no reason for a succession of what they regard as punitive measures, the six o'clock curfew in Jerusalem, the official army boycott of all Jewish shops and amusements places, the requisitioning of several of their business buildings for administration purposes. The freedom enjoyed by the Arabs rankles, too. The Jews claim, and offer a certain amount of evidence to support their contention, that some of the supplies of arms and ammunition found in Tel Aviv had been stored there long ago by Haganah, the Jewish self-defense corps, as a precaution against Arab uprisings, and had nothing to do with terrorist crimes. Even the most moderate Jews have now reached the point at which their horror at extremist outrages is not enough to impel them to cooperate with what they feel is an administration that, if not actively hostile, is certainly not sympathetic toward them either as a people or as a potential state.

Apprehension is as much a part of the Palestine atmosphere as the buff stones of the buildings that line its cities' streets or the incredibly pure blue of its skies. The people are obsessed by the question, Where will the next blow strike? Because arms were found under the synagogue in Tel Aviv, will all the holy places of Jerusalem now be ransacked? Not only the Jews are apprehensive. The British employees of the Public Information Office in Jerusalem have protested to their chiefs against staying in a building which they suspect may be next on the terrorists' list. Every day, from the windows of their offices, they see the shattered remains of the King David Hotel and the British flag flying at half-mast above it. They claim that barbed wire and sentries are not insurance enough. If, they say, the terrorists can pose as Arabs carrying milk cans or as RAF officers in RAF trucks, they can also pose as foreign correspondents, a considerable number of whom find it necessary to visit the Public Information Office every day.

The bona-fide foreign correspondents, drinking beer at their headquarters in the Eden Hotel, think that Haifa will be the next trouble spot. In the harbor there, two thousand or more illegal immigrants are waiting on four miserable ships, filthy craft that look like gypsy encampments because of the tattered tarpaulin tents set up on their decks. Half the passengers somehow manage to look not only hopeful but healthy, particularly the young women. The other half, especially the young men, look as if they'd escaped from the top layer of corpses in a Belsen ditch. Many of them doubtless did.

At the moment, two or three thousand more immigrants are believed to be at sea, heading for Haifa. The British are trying to figure out what to do about them. Twelve hundred others are already waiting at Athlit Camp, near Haifa, for admission. The British know that human beings cannot continue to live in the unspeakable conditions that exist on board these ships without serious danger of an epidemic of some sort. They know, too, that if they send the immigrants back to where they came from, the Jewish population of Palestine will react strongly, and that if they land all the new arrivals, the Arab population will rise. Moreover, they know that if they land the immigrants and then keep them behind barbed wire in camps month after month, they will be providing a breeding ground for terrorists.

The Tel Aviv operation is over and its people are again free. But after six in the evening, the Jewish part of Jerusalem is a dead city, echoing only to the rattle of Bren-gun carriers and armored cars. And on the road north from Tel Aviv, convoys of motorized equipment and men are streaming toward Haifa.

RIGGS:
WHERE
PSYCHIATRISTS LEARN

The house where the patients live is called the Inn: a white building, unpretentious but formal, too large for a private residence nowadays, too small for a hotel, in no way an institution. For the basic tenant of the Austen Riggs Center in Stockbridge, Massachusetts, is that the best way to care for the sick in mind is to keep them among the healthy, as a part of a living community to which they must try to relate themselves sooner or later.

Forty patients live in the Inn, each suffering from a different kind of psychoneurosis. They are not sick enough for a closed institution, but they are too ill to continue their ordinary lives while they are treated. They range from the teens to middle age, with the majority in their twenties and thirties.

If you saw them among you, as the natives of Stockbridge do every day, you would probably not find anything remarkable about them. Only a trained eye or an intuitive heart can single out the disturbed, can detect, through a way of walking or using the hands, through expressions of the eyes and mouth, which of us are trapped in a private prison. Without this insight, they are as you or I.

Riggs is a pilot plant, an institute of advanced study where some of the best psychiatrists in the country have the means, time, and privacy to find out what sickens the human mind and what can restore it. This is virtually impossible in a state institution, where one doctor must often "handle" four hundred patients. At Riggs there are four patients to one doctor.

Schizophrenia, anxiety, paranoia, fear, apathy, aggression, and masochism are manifested to varying degrees by some of the patients. Where do they start? The woman who flies from marriage into unreality, the brilliant youth who breaks down on the threshold of a successful career, an unmarried man or woman in middle age who searches forever for a home that has never existed, the husband who after ten years of a happy marriage feels an anguished compulsion to dress like a woman, a young girl who craves death, the woman who washes her hands all day and can touch nothing for fear of defilement — these were once able to live with themselves and with others, if not happily, then at least within the pattern of society. What pushed them out of this pattern, beyond the line?

The doctors at Riggs talk with humility before such mysteries. "We think we know some of the reasons, and we know some ways to help. The rest is unexplored territory. We don't even use the word 'cure,'" explained one staff member. "Even though a patient may leave us much better than he came, how can we tell that he is wholly cured? We can only say that he is 'markedly improved' or 'restored to his premorbid condition.' But we can never be sure that under stress the wounds will not open again."

No psychiatrist can apply automatically to one patient what he has learned from another. Each mind is a private world, although the winds that sweep through them may be universal. When people reach the breaking point or exceed it, they need a moratorium, a vacation from their former activities and environment. This period may be as short as a month or as long as two years, but without a respite the sickness can only feed and grow on itself. During meetings with doctors and visits with patients at Riggs, I was impressed by the high level of the painting and sculpture that was done as part of therapy. Apart from illuminating the condition of the patients, much of it could stand comparison with some of the work seen in contemporary galleries. (They also produce and act in plays before playing local audiences with a competence which, according to Clifford Odets, who saw one of his plays so performed in Stockbridge, is equal to that of any good amateur group.) Questions lingered long after my discussions — certainly not original inquiries, but vexing just the same.

There was talk of a man who was incapable of responding to therapy because he had no "conscience." What was conscience?

Why did more of the young show a need of psychiatric help?

What part did heredity play in mental illness? The doctors maintained that it was very slight, compared to environmental stresses, yet did not the constitutional factors in each human being affect environment?

Was not the psychiatrist, in his justifiable impatience with the questionable concept of "normality," in danger of directing his sympathy to the abnormal, accepting it as the natural product of our times?

On the defensive after long popular suspicion and misinterpretation, was not psychiatry becoming a religion, with doctors as priests and patients as disciples, and the world outside, the world of the so-called "normal" or balanced, an obtuse and unenlightened one?

One young doctor at Riggs said it best, without quite answering these queries. "If we can change neurotic suffering into common unhappiness, we feel we have accomplished a great deal."

COMING OF AGE
REPORT ON
THE HODSON CENTER

The big room was filled with light from the tall windows, so you could see the old people clearly. There were about a hundred, most of them seated at tables. Four or five groups of old men were playing cards, some were just sitting and looking, a tableful of women chatted, and there was movement in the form of a line toward the cafeteria window at one end. The atmosphere, wholly tangible, was of bustle and contentment. As Gertrude Landau, director of the William Hodson Community Center in the Bronx, took me around, the old faces were raised in interest, a number nodded and smiled. Only the cardplayers seemed to need no distraction; most of their heads remained bent.

An old woman, poorly dressed, came up to us. In a very heavy accent she said, "This is my home. This is my family. Was business-woman, work hard, husband, children, then depression, everything gone, ruin. Now I am nobody, worth nothing....But this is my home."

Miss Landau said, "That's not true, Mrs. Kranek, you *are* somebody. Come and talk to me soon, and I'll tell you who you are!"

We left the big room and went upstairs into a shop filled with tools and lathes and sewing machines. "They can go on with their former skills here," said Miss Landau, "or learn new ones. Look, by the window there, one of our real characters." Sitting at a workbench was a man who looked like a very old Popeye. He was bent over, whittling something, and his undershot jaw was working steadily on a wad of tobacco.

We came a little closer and saw that he was putting the finishing touches to a filigree fan of great delicacy. We were about to inspect it and meet him when he got up to reach for another tool and made the most astonishing motions, flapping his arms as if he were about to take off. Instead he keeled partly over and sat down heavily on the floor. Before anyone could assist him, he had pulled himself painfully up to a chair, breathing heavily.

"Arteriosclerosis," said Miss Landau. "He has practically no sense of balance. He's all right once he gets started. It's the transitions that are tough—you know, sitting to standing, standing to walking. He comes here alone every day from Flatbush, makes two subway changes and a bus." In answer to my amazement and alarm, she smiled. "Yes, it used to unnerve us, too, but he's managed so far. He wouldn't miss the Center for anything. He's something of an old rascal, but we love his work and so does he, and we're proud of him."

Miss Landau opened the door to a smaller room filled with sound. A younger woman was playing the piano and about ten old people seated in two rows of chairs were accompanying her with instruments: triangles, cymbals, marimbas, drums. They would accent the rhythm as she did, their faces alight and happy, although the old man in charge of the drum was tense with the responsibility of his beat.

"Our music class is very popular," said Miss Landau. "They have an added incentive because they play for the birthday parties we have every month and for special occasions, so it isn't just time-passing. They have to perform."

We crossed the hall again into another room where a barber's chair, basin, and mirror stood between the high windows. A tall old man in an immaculate white coat was doing a highly professional job on another old man. I noticed that the barber was very grave and never spoke.

"Mr. Santucci has been in this country sixty years, but he's never really learned English," explained Miss Landau. "He used to be a very successful barber on Wall Street because he never made conversation."

After Mr. Santucci had brushed off his customer, a rather

untidy old woman with a long gray bob came up and asked him to cut her hair. He shook his head. Upset, she turned to Miss Landau and asked why he refused.

"Mr. Santucci thinks women are never satisfied, and so he cuts only men's hair. He thinks that if he cut yours you would not like it and then it would be his fault." This masterly interpretation of what Mr. Santucci did not say seemed to satisfy the woman, who shrugged and left.

We made one more brief excursion through the shabby corridors to a cluttered locker room to look at some paintings by members of the Center, and in so doing passed a tiny space no larger than a closet where four old people sat playing canasta. Miss Landau teased them for being so exclusive in their immoral pursuit, and they all chuckled like children caught stealing jam. "This is about the only privacy they can get," she said.

Among the paintings were some extraordinary decorative watercolors by a Mr. Piltz, Persian in the brilliance of their color and the intricacy of their design in which birds, trees, flowers, and rivers were fancifully intertwined. "He is one of our real talents," said Miss Landau. "Someday we hope to exhibit his work downtown."

Then we returned to the cafeteria to have lunch (a good thick soup, sardine salad, coffee, fruit, and cake) and to talk about Hodson.

I had confessed that I had not expected to find happiness here. I had come to this place in the Bronx recoiling in apprehension from the smell of age, the apparition of infirmity, apathy, and resignation. All of us, I think, are weighed down with a sense of guilt about the old. We do not cherish them as our parents did; we seem to have little room for them in our hearts or lives. Mistakenly we have come to believe that they need us far more than we need them.

Raw weather and ugly streets around the Center were both depressing, in no way relieved by the sight of the ponderous old building at Tremont and Third Avenue, a relic of the 1890s. When I glanced at a black couple entering the main door arm-in-arm, Miss

Landau said, "This was the old Borough Hall. The marriage license bureau is still here, and a lot of other things. We have only a few rooms in the building."

Then came the revelation of old people finding their place together, their own, where they belonged. The hundreds who come to Hodson cannot be so different from the tens of thousands who live in this city. Many of them, especially the men, live in furnished rooms, alone, on old-age relief. After working all of their lives, they have nothing to do. Degeneration of the spirit and of the tissues takes its relentless, interacting course as they either sit their hours out in chronic depression or haunt clinics and hospitals, not so much to cure their ailments as to have attention, to *speak* to somebody. At Hodson there are many old people who still live with their relatives in comparative security. But to read their histories is to know that there is hardly one who does not feel a burden; unwanted, useless, dependent. There is hardly one who is not aware of the tensions this feeling produces, of the fact that the younger people keep them out of duty or pity, even if love is present. And so all but the very wise become difficult to themselves and others, either straining for that sense of importance and worth they feel they have earned and been denied, or giving up and waiting until they can die.

The Center opened in 1943 to provide "leisure time activities for the older person." Hodson has a membership of 1,500. About 250 come in a day, some every day, others a few times a week. They range from 60 to 94, with most of them in their seventies. Nearly 85 percent of the Hodson members are foreign-born. Jews predominate. The average level of school attendance was the fifth grade, and a good number of those at Hodson are learning English there in special classes.

It is significant that most of the older people came to the Center not immediately after retirement, but after many years of living alone. In a five-year span at the Center, only ten have sought admission to a home for the aged, three of whom later returned to live alone and spend their days at the Center. There has not been a single admission to a mental hospital from among the membership.

Hodson is open every day from nine till five. To many of the men, this span is a substitute for the business day, to others for the club. Even those who have families find that they cherish this freedom to be themselves as they were themselves. For the women, Hodson means family, gossip, companionship. Here, for both sexes, is the audience they crave.

A lot of them, when they first come to Hodson, are timid, withdrawn, insecure. Then gradually, through cards or music class or dramatics or committee work (there are lots of committees), they begin to emerge, make contact, stir old skills and dreams.

Here in case histories from a book on the Center by Miss Landau and Susan H. Kubie, is the sort of things that goes on:

Mr. Sullivan was a tense, somewhat rigid and extremely reserved man who came to the Center daily but remained aloof from the others and spent most of his time reading or listening to the radio.... One day he showed her [a staff worker] some verses he had written. She suggested that others at the Center might like to meet weekly to hear his poems and to read poetry to each other. It came about quite naturally that he took the lead in the first such poetry meeting by reading one of his own.

Her [a Mrs. Figler's] reading is barely intelligible. She herself does not understand the selections she chooses at random, according to length, from the anthologies available. Yet she persists, reading in a low voice, hands shaking with nervousness, and finishes with a quick little bob to the audience. She is rewarded with approving comments on "her effort and her progress." It is perhaps true that her limitations, plus her persistence, afford them group satisfaction....

Mr. Sobolski is blind and first came to the sessions as a listener. But presently he was impelled to bring selections he had typed in Braille so that he could also contribute. When his turn came the group listened in silence, watching with fascination as his fingers slid over the raised dots of his paper. The applause was heartwarming and tremendous. . . .

Let no one assume, because of the many happy responses, that sweetness and light are the order of every Hodson day. A hundred or more old people thrown together, however voluntarily, can engender the same frictions that stir other groups, child or adult. Competitiveness, jealousy, pique, hurt feelings, obsessions of inferiority, these can and do explode periodically. Mrs. Greenberg is angry at Mrs. Miller because "she throws her education around." Mr. Jason is annoyed because an art instructor spends more time with Mr. Blau than with him. The whole discussion group is outraged because Mr. F., aggressive and long-winded, has brought up an unpopular subject. Nearly all the members who are not habitual cardplayers look down on those who are, because they "don't do anything for the Center."

Some of the explosions are more comic than tragic, for example a quarrel between two newlyweds in their eighties (they met at the Center, and the license bureau was conveniently downstairs) in which Mrs. Y threw a brick at Mr. Y outside on the grounds, missing him. Miss Landau retrieved the brick and put it in her safe and told Mrs. Y to come and ask her for it when she wanted to use it again. Mrs. Y didn't.

At the Hodson Center, the old wait not for death, but for each day to come.

U.N.:
THE FINE ART
OF CORRIDOR
SITTING

Established reporters of the international scene need not read this. They know their way around. The small sensations of power that a press card gives (it gets you past the first guard) ebb quickly once you are within the United Nations. Everyone else seems to know where they are going, particularly the moving belts of people on the escalators, passing each other diagonally and gravely in a purposeful cross-rhythm. The bureaucrats know what is in their briefcases. Stenographers know where to get their coffee. The Indian ladies in saris have no doubt that they are women.

The press section, or bullpen, is bright and large, well-planned, with no city-room raffishness. Some of the correspondents there looked more intelligent and more ravaged than others, and I assumed they were French. I saw few women in the bullpen: one stiffly encased in a tailored suit with a face like the *New Jersey* and a bag full of releases; another in a skirt and cap obviously woven by herself, lugging a large, congested feed bag made of matching material.

Correspondents formed lines for tickets to the Security Council. I was passed over the first time, having lost out to a reporter from a prominent paper. The second time I preempted the ticket of another big-paper correspondent too busy to look at delegates. Once through the press entrance of the Security Council, I grabbed one of the front seats. This was wrong; important correspondents take the back seats, higher up. It was a rousing and dramatic session, and I watched the faces of the diverse delegates. Sir Leslie Munro of New Zealand was a mastiff. Hervé Alphand of France needed only a tumbling white wig to make his pink imperious face and pouched eyes into an eighteenth-century royal image. Henry Cabot Lodge looked, as always, like an all-American boy. Krishna Menon, sitting in the observers' section, combined the qualities of a dark Savonarola, a molten Lucifer, and the Bad Fairy in a ballet. Dr. Tingfu Tsiang of Nationalist China resembled a pained frog. Whenever he spoke, the others would look at him as if he were a rare and curious specimen, the last of its kind.

At one point Mrs. Oswald B. Lord (Human Rights) walked across the putting-lawn carpet to confer, a red velvet clamp on her hand. This prompted a bearded Scandinavian next to me to remark in a hoarse whisper that just before Mrs. Lord was to have made a speech the previous day on the Nationality of Married Women to the General Assembly, a young lady had rushed up to her with a box. Mrs. Lord opened it, replaced the hat she had on with the one she took out, and mounted the stand.

Mercifully soon, a big-paper correspondent suggested that I sit with him higher up, where I could see better. I used my new vantage point to study the mural in the background. There were little groups of people with chains on their legs straining toward the light at the top of the picture, and at the bottom a large strange bird, surely unknown to Audubon, sitting on a pile of what seemed to be automobile parts. I was just thinking that I had seldom seen a worse painting anywhere when a distinguished foreign correspondent across the aisle passed me a note saying, "Who painted that *splendid* mural, and why?"

There was a lot of note passing, in the collegiate manner. When Sir Pierson Dixon was making one of his tutorial speeches, ruminating on the "tolerant and forgiving" virtues of the British people, saying that his delegation would vote for the admission of Bad Nations, too, in the hope that they might become Good, one note fluttered up, reading "And quiet flowed the Don."

For informal delegate viewing, I recommend the wide, curving corridors outside the Security Council chamber. The best place is in the middle, where you can catch the delegates on their way to and from the North and South Lounges. If you need quotable items, correspondents in the bullpen will oblige. Lodge, in particular, seems to worry them. A Swiss told me that the trouble with Lodge was that he was playing poker while everybody else played chess.

In a corner of the curve of the General Assembly Building, there is a small place called the Meditation Room. It is windowless and rectangular, but rounded at one end, curtained from floor to ceiling in off-white, carpeted in off-white, and lit by beams from spotlights in the ceiling. About twenty armchairs of American pine with barrel-stave backs, five to a row, face the curved end of the room, in the center of which is a polished reddish tree trunk about four feet high and three feet across. On top of that is a cluster of philodendron in a receptacle. A separate shaft of light is directed on this, as if it were significant.

The U.N. information desk told me that this room was conceived and executed by the Laymen's Movement for a Christian World, as a place where delegates might pray or ponder in peace. And as it was for the use of scores of nations and many religions, care had been taken to avoid any symbol that might offend any believer. Even the United Nations flag, once there, had to go. So now there were the trunk, the plant, and the chairs.

It seemed to me that the core of our greatest trouble lay here, in the whiteness and shapelessness of this padded cell for the soul. We had found, finally, that only nothing could please all. The terrifying thing about the Meditation Room was that it made no statement whatsoever. In its opacity and constriction, it could not even act as a reflector of thought.

In a provocative book entitled *Must You Conform?*, psychiatrist Robert Lindner presents one cure for this spiritual leukemia:

"I suggest that the answer. . . lies in the mobilization and implementation of the instinct of rebellion. We must, in short, become acquainted with our protestant nature and learn how to use it in our daily lives, how to express it, how to infuse it throughout all levels of our culture, and how to nourish it in our young.

If we don't, presumably the spirit of man will be both represented and worshiped in rooms like this one at the U.N., a quiet place of detachment where we can look at the philodendron in the light from nowhere and meditate on nothing. Or play poker.

THE MURDER OF
IN HO OH

*(Awarded the
Certificate of
Recognition in the
National Brotherhood
Media Award
Competition)*

The crime was appalling because it was wholly without motive.
It might have happened to anyone who crossed Hamilton Avenue at
Thirty-sixth Street in Philadelphia at nine o'clock on the evening of
April 25, 1958. There is nothing particularly sinister about the street
or the neighborhood. Heavy-leaved trees line the sidewalk and half-
obscure the wood-and-stucco houses with their porches and pillars,
slightly melancholy for lack of paint and an air of past gentility. Most
are now filled with roomers: students from the University of Pennsylvania, ten blocks or so away, and white and colored people of
modest means.

A Korean student named In Ho Oh lived with his aunt and
uncle in a small and bare apartment in a corner house. His purpose
in leaving it that night was to mail a letter in the mailbox diagonally
across the street. His misfortune was to be on the street when eleven
teen-age blacks came by after having been turned away from a
neighborhood dance — some, it seems, because of "improper attire"
and some for lack of the admission price of sixty-five cents. According to newspaper reports the following day, they met other youths
and told them what had happened. "At that point," a Juvenile Aid
officer said, "these kids were ready to fight and probably would have
attacked the first person they met on the street."

At least seven of the boys involved set upon the small, slight
Korean student and beat him to death with a lead pipe, fists, shoes,

and a black-jack. When he was a bloody pulp on the sidewalk, one of them is said to have shouted, "I've got his wallet. There's no money in it." Then they ran away. In Ho Oh died ten minutes later.

For years men like Director Maurice Fagan of the Fellowship Commission in Philadelphia and many others in Jewish, Quaker, Protestant, and Catholic groups in Philadelphia have been trying — with some success — to educate their people in three concepts: that the answer to the brutality of crime is not brutality of law, for violence merely begets violence; that delinquency is bred not of race but of acute economic and social depression that disintegrates the family unit; and that if the incidence of black crime is high in the city, the deprivations of the black community and the indifference of their established neighbors has much to do with it. Of the half-million Negroes in Philadelphia, the majority live in squalor.

"After this," Fagan said, "we have been set back ten years. The attitudes have hardened: black against white, white against black. Compassion has been replaced by fear. And you cannot blame people," he said reluctantly, "for being afraid."

The murder of In Ho Oh was indeed enough to cause shock and abhorence as well as fear. And though the nature of the victim of a murder should not be a measure of the nature of the act, in this case the qualities of the young Korean brought the horror of the crime and its perpetrators into sharper focus.

His Uncle Ki Hang Oh and his young Aunt Za Young Oh remember every moment of the day he was killed and the night after it and the many nightmares of the next few weeks. Ki Hang, a stocky man of thirty-seven, is working for a doctorate in Assyriology at Dropsie College and has had a full-time job besides to support himself, Za Young, and their two children, who live with their grandparents in Korea. His young wife arrived only five months ago from Pusan to join her husband and study singing at the University of Pennsylvania. She speaks little English, but she often corrected or amplified her husband's account in soft Korean, which he then translated for my benefit.

"He was so happy that day," said Ki Hang. "I remember him that morning, so neatly dressed—he never wore sport clothes, always very formal and neat, with his hair oiled and his shoes polished, and his clean white shirt and tie.

"I think that he was happy because at last he did not have to work so hard at night. He was always tired before; you know it is tiring to study all day and work all night. My nephew, first he ran an elevator in a bank, and then lately they gave him other work, lighter work, and he had more time to study. Also he was happy because he liked his studies in political science more than at first. You know, he wished to be a statesman in Korea, and we all knew he would be a wonderful statesman. He wanted so much to help his people."

In Ho, I learned, had been first in his class at night school in Seoul and one of the top three at the Seoul National University. He came to the United States as an exchange student on a scholarship and was graduated in philosophy from Eastern Baptist College in 1957.

"Perhaps," said his uncle, "when I speak of my nephew I make him too beautiful," and then, correcting himself, "too nice." But all who knew In Ho said the same things of him: that he was brilliant, shy, kind, perceptive, and full of great promise. He was, as all his family were and are, a practicing and dedicated Christian. he had a clear vision of what he wanted to be and do, and both images merged with the future of his people.

"My nephew," said Ki Hang, "did not believe in violence, he did not understand violence. If somebody would hit him he would not think of defending himself." He did not add that In Ho had neither time nor chance on that night in April, even if the thought of defense had occurred.

The uncle then spoke of that night. He and his wife were resting on their beds, exhausted after the day's work. They heard In Ho leave his room and go out, and thought he was leaving for his job at the Provident Tradesmens Bank. Some time later they heard a knock on the door and Mrs. Oh went to answer it. It was dark and a man was outside and asked, "Does a Chinese or a Korean live with you here?" Then there were other people and police cars and policemen and lights, and Mrs. Oh became more and more confused and fearful and went to rouse her husband. When he came to the door a policeman showed him a ball-point pen and asked, "Does this belong to your nephew?" Ki Hang said "Yes"; In Ho had just bought several like it. And they told him what had happened.

"I lay on my bed then and could not rise. I could do nothing. I was overwhelmed. I could not move." So the uncle and aunt lay in a trance of horror while their friend, fellow student, and neighbor, Y. C. Kim, spoke for them to the police and then went with them to identify what was left of In Ho.

The Ohs were a prominent family in North Korea, where they had lived for generations before they fled from the Russians to the south after the Second World War; a large, affluent, and public-spirited clan who managed miraculously to preserve their family unity — in spirit at least — through half a century of Japanese occupation, Communist harassment, flight, dislocation, the Korean War, and all the successive dangers, deprivations, and deaths these events had brought upon them. Ki Hang himself went to high school in Manchuria, to a university in Japan, then back to South Korea during the war, where he was taken prisoner by the North Koreans and held for several months.

"I have seen many horrible things in these years, he said, "but not anything so horrible as what occurred to my nephew, for it had no meaning. I know of the Japanese atrocities and I know they were horrible. But they were not without reason: the Japanese did this for their country and their Emperior. The boys who killed my nephew had no reason." Yet when Ki Hang mentioned the black boys, he did so with a strange detachment. Not once did he use the word "murder," and the phrase "when my nephew died" came most often to his lips.

The shock waves that hit Philadelphia were felt thousands of miles away. Although Ki Hang Oh had immediately sent a cable to

In Ho's parents in Seoul telling them of the tragedy, it reached them only after they had read of it in the Korean papers. They telephoned him: "Can this possibly be true?"

By this time, the conscience of Philadelphia made itself felt. The press and Mayor Richardson Dilworth gave full expression to the surge of shame and horror. Because In Ho had been a civilian interpreter with the U.S. Army during the Korean War, two women volunteers in the local Red Cross chapter undertook to provide communication between the family in Korea and the family in Philadelphia, and they assisted in the painful and complex processes of In Ho's funeral and the disposition of his body. At first the Ohs felt that it should be returned to Korea so that the ancient rituals involving his parents' presence at the interment could be consummated. A maze of obstacles, including prolonged delay in transporting the casket, made this impossible, and it was decided in family council to cremate his remains and ship his ashes for burial there. But this decision in turn was rescinded by In Ho's parents. This letter made their reasons clear:

Pusan, Korea

Director
Philadelphia Red Cross

Dear Sir:

We, the parents of In Ho Oh, on behalf of our whole family, deeply appreciate the expressions of sympathy you have extended to us at this time. In Ho had almost finished the preparation needed for the achievement of his ambition, which was to serve his people and nation as a Christian statesman. His death by an unexpected accident leaves that ambition unachieved.

When we heard of his death, we could not believe the news was true, for the shock was so unexpected and sad, but now we find that it is an undeniable fact that In Ho has been killed by a gang of black boys whose souls were not saved and in whom human nature is paralyzed. We are sad now, not only because of In Ho's unachieved future, but also because of the unsaved souls and paralyzed human nature of the murderers.

We thank God that He has given us a plan whereby our sorrow is being turned into Christian purpose. It is our hope that we may somehow be instrumental in the salvation of the souls, and in giving life to the human nature of the murderers. Our family has met together and we have decided to petition that the most generous treatment possible within the laws of your government be given to those who have committed this criminal action without knowing what it would mean to him who has been sacrificed, to his family, to his friends, and to his country.

In order to give evidence of our sincere hope contained in this petition our whole family has decided to save money to start a fund to be used for the religious, educational, vocational, and social guidance of the boys when they are released. In addition, we are daring to hope that we can do something to minimize such juvenile criminal actions which are to be found, not only in your country, but also in Korea, and, we are sure, everywhere in the world.

About the burial of the physical body of him who has been sacrificed; we hope that you could spare a piece of land in your country and bury it there, for your land, too, is homeland for Christians and people of the democratic society, and it is our sincere hope that thus we will remember your people, and you will remember our people, and that both you and we will more vitally sense an obligation for the better guidance of juvenile delinquents whose souls are unsaved, and whose human natures are paralyzed. We hope in this way to make his tomb a monument which will call attention of people to this cause. We think this is a way to give life to the dead, and to the murderers, and to keep you and us closer in Christian love and fellowship.

We are not familiar with your customs and you may find something hard to understand in what we are trying to say and do.

Please interpret our hope and idea with Christian spirit and in the light of democratic principles. We have dared to express our hope with a spirit received from the Gospel of our Savior Jesus Christ who died for our sins.

May God bless you, your people, and particularly the boys who killed our son and kinsman.

Ki Byang Oh (father)
President, Yung-Chin Industrial Company
Shin Wynn H. Oh (mother)

This letter was signed also by two uncles, two aunts, five sisters, two brothers, and nine cousins.

The funeral services were held in a small chapel in West Philadelphia. To represent his parents, In Ho's older uncle, Ki Song Oh, who was completing his master of arts degree in international law at the university in Austin, Texas, was flown to Philadelphia so that he could attend the ceremony — with the aid and resources, once more, of the Red Cross chapter. There were about fifty mourners — Korean fellow students of In Ho, his professors, close friends, and community leaders. A large number of blacks lived in the neighborhood, but no blacks were to be seen. Fearfully and silently they peered through their windows at the coffin and the mourners.

Mayor Dilworth spoke and wept. The handsome, war-toughened ex-marine said in a broken voice, "It is a horrible thing that this could happen in our city." At the close of the service he stood apart from the others, looking down at the sealed casket.

The young Korean finally came to rest in the consecrated ground of the Old Pine Street Presbyterian Church in the company of Philadelphia's honored Americans.

Though their nephew's body was in peace and the boys who killed him had been arraigned and the good people of the city were offering help and kindness in every turn, Ki Hang Oh and his wife could no longer bear to remain in the street where In Ho Oh had died. They kept seeing his face and hearing his voice. And there were mysterious telephoned threats, the psychotic wake of crime and horror. Police were stationed to protect the Ohs and follow them everywhere, but still they felt they had to move away.

After a fruitless search for a shelter within their means, a director of the Red Cross chapter offered to take them into his home. "Even here," he said, "on the top floor, with my family around them and police outside, they were filled with fear. I could hear Mrs. Oh pacing the floor of her room at four in the morning, night after night."

"We are very careful now—very careful," said Ki Hang Oh.

And what of the cause of their terror and their loss, the boys who had killed? The police had rounded most of them up within a few hours of the crime. "Our Gang Control Squad," said the inspector in charge of the Juvenile Aid bureau, "knows all the gangs in each neighborhood and we had plenty of clues."

Since the case, to open June 23 with separate trials for the defendants, is *sub judice*, details concerning the youths cannot be released at this point. But already published are these facts about the nine being held. Their ages range from fifteen to nineteen, and they come from the lowest income group in the city, from broken homes and slum neighborhoods. Several of them have records of previous arrests. Two bear proud American names: Douglas MacArthur Clark and Franklin Marshall. One, the eldest, is retarded. And in refutation of a popular theory that newcomers from the South are the root of the trouble, all the boys were Philadelphia-born, though their parents may have come from the South. In speaking of this migration, Director of Parole Dr. John Otto Reinemann suggested that boys of this age, black or white, suffered particularly from parental neglect, for their mothers had entered defense plants during the war, leaving them to a life on the streets without guidance, home, or family. "These boys were born, you see, in the 1940s."

Philadelphia feels an almost personal shame for them; an emotion apparently alien to New York, which is too big, too complex, and too diffuse to feel responsibility for the crimes committed daily on its streets. It may also be that Philadelphia's conscience has been prodded chiefly by the traditions of its Quaker and Jewish groups. For although the city has bred individuals of great distinction and service of other faiths and affiliations, there is a cohesion among the Friends and the Jews that gives them particular strength.

But for the average citizen, the shame felt for these boys was coupled not so much with a sense of responsibility for their condition as with a loathing that found its quickest release in fear and hysteria. The first stunned reaction to the Christian charity the Ohs had shown changed from incredulity and admiration to a mounting demand for vengeful action. Although the black papers, often shrill with their own hysteria of resentment and blame of whites, exaggerated when they wrote of a "pre-trial 'lynch atmosphere,'" the editor of the Philadelphia *Courier* spoke of the simple truth when he said: "Most tragic of all regarding civil stability is that when crimes are committed by Negro youths, public indignation turns upon the Negro race, sparing none."

It has also turned, with fury, on all forms of sociological explanation, on all efforts at understanding basic causes, at all corrective measures that are not immediate and merciless. "The public," said Mr. Fagan sadly, "Is willing to spend unlimited funds for whipping posts, in spite of the fact that there is conclusive proof that 'the works' don't work any more than 'softness' does." And the inspector of Juvenile Aid himself admitted that strong-arm methods by the police alone were of little avail.

"We did a month's experiment with gangs of delinquents," he said, "harassing them all the time, arresting them, sitting on their necks, throwing them in jail for the smallest offenses, and at the end of that time the incidence of crimes among them only increased. We found that the only way we could get anywhere was through the active cooperation of the community where they lived—with their teachers and their parents, with civic groups and social workers. And for two years now we have had special officers on our force who have been trained in community relations at the University of Pennsylvania.

"It's a slow process, and there are no quick answers. But we seem to have made some progress in one area at least, and that's in the use of weapons. Ever since our judges have clamped down hard on kids for the mere possession of weapons, you don't see so many. They're afraid to get caught with them. The boys in this case mostly used hands and feet—except for pop bottles and that one blackjack."

The public may demand a quick end to its fears and an assurance of safety through harsh means; the district attorney may, as he has promised, exact utmost penalties for this hideous crime. But the wise men, the good men, and the brave men of the town know better—the mayor himself, the Juvenile Aid inspector, the director of paroles, the head of the new and shining Youth Study Center where the delinquent boys and girls are held before they are brought to trial or returned to their homes.

In a broadcast soon after the murder the mayor spoke on the whole subject of delinquency in Philadelphia. He mentioned the flood of mail he had received urging immediate and repressive action and underlaid with racial animus, and he said, among other things: "I think it is helpful to give a specific example of the terrible harm that is reaped upon a community by inhuman, repressive measures." And he told of the way Blacks lived in Johannesburg and were treated there. "Any Negro found on the street at night is shot on sight. Yet, today, Johannesburg has the highest incidence of Negro crimes of violence of any city in the world, and the white population does not dare venture on the streets at night without armed protection. I just do not think that we can emphasize enough that man's inhumanity to man simply results in increased violence and evil."

In discussing solutions, the mayor said: "The fundamental reason so many juveniles have been released on probation is that our state is unfortunately almost a hundred years behind the times in providing the essential facilities for dealing with juvenile problems ...today we have no facility whatsoever in the state to which mentally disturbed or backward girls can be sent. There is absolutely no facility operated by the state for mentally disturbed or backward boys under sixteen years of age. There is absolutely no state institution where juveniles who are just starting to turn bad and need a good sharp, short lesson can be sent...." And there was no place at all where those who have served their sentences can be prepared for a return to freedom: a sort of decompression chamber for emergence into normal society.

"I myself," he said later, "have appeared at four successive sessions of the legislature to urge the necessary appropriations for these essential facilities, but have been told that there has been no evidence of any citizen interest; on the contrary, that the citizens are demanding a decrease in so-called welfare expenditures."

And as if to disprove this charge and to answer the flood of questions from a presumably awakened citizenry as to what they themselves could do to stem this tide of youthful crime, the mayor listed twenty-two organizations and activities that an individual could join in the fight against delinquency. The broadcast is estimated to have reached many tens of thousands in the city. Ninety-four Philadelphians volunteered their services.

Although the mayor took pains to make clear that the high rate of crime among Philadelphia's half-million Blacks was an inevitable result of the appalling conditions in which many were forced to live and the attendant human disintegrations, he did not absolve the Black community of its share of guilt.

"There is also a regrettable scarcity of leadership in the Black communities in the large cities. That is largely due to the fact that only some ninety years have elapsed since the days of slavery and very little opportunity has been open to them in fields which create leadership. ...I think the one real criticism that can be leveled at some of the important elements of the Negro community is that they demand, as they should, their rights as first-class citizens, but at the same time seek to retain the privileges and special considerations of a distinctly minority group. They must do more to help themselves..."

Mrs. Oh had only this to say of the boys who killed her nephew:

"Not one of their families wrote to share our sorrow. In our country people in their position would have done so." She might also have added that no matter how grinding their poverty, Asian mothers do not leave their children on the street but preserve, above all, the family unit. It is an established fact that of all the minorities in this country the Chinese have the lowest crime rate.

"Our main purpose now," said Mr. Fagan of the Fellowship Commission, "Is to keep some line of communication open between whites and blacks, so that they can at least still talk to each other. If that is lost, everything else goes too."

Yet much has been done since In Ho was killed — by the people who always act when they are needed, in war or peace. The mayor immediately set up a scholarship fund, contributing the first $100 himself, for a Korean student at the University of Pennsylvania, and it has passed the $4,000 mark.

The Red Cross chapter and the Provident Tradesmens Bank and Trust Company where In Ho worked have established a fund for Ki Hang Oh and his wife, so that they can finish their studies and he his thesis without his forty-eight-hour-a-week job to consume his time, and so that they can return sooner to Korea to join their children and teach. "My wife will give concerts there," he said, "to raise more money for the memory of In Ho and his fund." Already $1,700 has been collected from private citizens for this purpose. Their former neighbors have collected money in In Ho's name for the U.N. International Children's Emergency Fund, to provide milk in Korea.

The Ohs are profoundly grateful for what has been done for them by the people of Philadelphia, the groups of citizens that are the core of its conscience, the compassionate ones. They cannot understand the vengeful rage of others who suffered no loss.

And when you ask Ki Hang what — if he had the power — he would do for these boys who killed, how he would actually implement his family's purpose of guidance and mercy for them, he only smiles and says: "You know we do not think of social problems. We are very simple. We have very simple ideas. We do not believe in hate or violence. We believe in the Christian spirit, and God's love."

God's love may not satisfy the people who live in fear. It provides no practical answer to Philadelphia's pressing troubles. In itself it is certainly no program of action.

But in their simplicity the Ohs may have made us wonder just how Christian those people are who cry for retribution and demand violence as a counter to violence, and just how well the people of the enlightened West take care of their own children.

A MORNING AFTER
IN NOTTING HILL

Soon after the first race riots in London, I spent a few hours one morning walking through the streets where they took place in the company of an English writer who is familiar with the scenes and the people. From Ladbroke Grove to Paddington, from Harrow Road to Kensington Park Row, we looked and wondered.

The neighborhood is not cause enough, dreary and poor as it is. Though the plaster peels from the once-respectable cream houses, and the smell that comes out of their black doorways is the familiar gas of poverty — airlessness, old bedding, sweat, urine, old fats — the streets are still incomparably better than any typical Puerto Rican slum in New York or the bad sections of Harlem. In Notting Hill there are trees and small patches of garden, however trodden and shabby, and the sky is broadly visible over the low houses. The high brownstones of New York with their scaffolding of fire escapes, the brown littered stoops, the filthy gutters, the total absence of green and growing life — all these are far more oppressive. Even the most bleak and squalid dead end on Notting Hill is swept of litter. It is not the worst place to live.

As for the people there, most were at work that morning, except for women marketing or pushing prams and a few men walking purposefully, as if to idle might attract attention. The atmosphere was one of suspenseful quiet; a lull that did not seem particularly chastened.

There were some colored people about: Jamaican housewives, neatly dressed, and at least three black men who wore bandages on head or hand or arm. On three occasions we passed the kind of youths, walking in pairs or threes, who seemed from all accounts to have caused most of the troubles. They were not Teddy Boys either in age or dress. They simply looked like tough young rowdies in their twenties. But they were quiet enough this particular morning.

We crossed a street to speak with a colored man on the other side. He had a light skin, a small neat mossy beard, and a cultivated voice, accented as only Jamaicans speak. He carried a small zipper bag full of groceries and vegetables. My friend introduced him as Roy.

"Man," said Roy, "this whole thing is absurd, completely absurd. Why do they do a thing like that, I ask you, why? Why now? Why us?"

My friend asked him about the riots themselves, and Roy said: "There's something behind it, there's somebody behind it, and money too. It didn't just happen. I've lived in this neighborhood for four years and I know most of the people by sight, but I didn't recognize a single face in the lot of the bully boys that came riding through here, fighting the colored."

"Did they do anything to you, Roy?"

He smiled. "I got off the street when the trouble started, but they smashed all the windows in the house where I live while I was at the club.

"And as for that," he continued, "we were sitting around at the club having a perfectly quiet evening drinking beer, talking, when the police came trampling down the stairs like a bunch of Teddy Boys, shouting. Couldn't they have come in quietly? Did they have to scare us half to death?"

He went on then to give instances of police hostility to colored people in general, whether guilty or innocent of any offense. "They're not for us," he protested; "they're for the others. They've arrested a lot of our boys on no evidence at all."

Roy shook his head, his face serious. "It's sad and it's terrible. I never thought it would happen here—never. But I'll tell you one thing: if those gangs attack us again we'll be ready for them. Our boys are organizing for it—they won't wait for the police to take care of the bullies. They'll handle them themselves, no matter what happens.

"As for me," said Roy, "I stay off the streets at night now. And

I've closed my shop because that street's not a fit place for any man now."

We left him and went on walking and talking, "I think Roy's right," said my friend, "that these outbursts were not spontaneous but directed, and that some plan is behind them. I have no proof yet, but I'm pretty certain Mosley has a hand in it. It smells more fascist than Communist to me, though the Commies are undoubtedly making hay with it."

This is the assumption of most informed people here. "We feel," said Barbados Prime Minister Dr. Hugh Cummins, while on a visit to London, "that the average Englishman doesn't explode into intense racial feeling, and we think there is something deeper behind this."

Yet the average Englishman living side by side with the West Indian immigrants has his own resentments, legitimate or fancied, and they follow the universal pattern of all areas where newcomers move in on previously established residents. Low as the community may be, the immigrants pull it down still lower. Overcrowding, dirt, noise, lax morals — these, say many unwilling neighbors, are what the colored newcomers bring. The vices and privileges of a few are ascribed to the many: "They keep white girls and live off them"; "They run houses of prostitution"; "They drive flashy cars while we have none"; "They take our jobs from us." No matter how proportionately small are the evidences of such offenses among the entire immigrant population, which numbers no more than about five thousand in the Notting Hill area, they produce an unrest that smolders under the surface, ready for conflagration.

And as usual, sex is the igniter. A "singularly tough" young Teddy Boy told a reporter on one of the days when riots took place, "There's a yobbo and his shackie in there. I was going to see they got paid, but some slag leaked to the coppers." A shackie is a white girl who goes to live with a colored man. A yobbo is a black pimp. A slag is a white girl who lives with or is friendly with colored people of either sex. The rest seems clear enough.

What might not be clear to Americans is that for white English girls of the lowest social and economic conditions it is a step up to live with a well-heeled colored man, for the simple fact of her own color brings her a status she never had before.

I suspect that the English will be slower now to recoil with horror at Little Rock, not because they condemn it less, but because they condemn themselves more. Now they know what we feel like.

DIALOGUE
OF A TOURIST
IN RUSSIA
(NOVEMBER 10, 1960)

The view from the twenty-seventh floor of the Hotel Ukraine in Moscow should be exciting, for the eye has no impediment: from one window I could see the curve of the Moscow River beyond freight yards; from the other I could see the major artery of Kuznetsov Street, and far away, on the only rise, the imposing complex of the University on the Lenin Hills.

But there was a terrible loneliness about this view. The river was dead, without shipping. The acres of identical yellow apartment houses in unbroken rows seemed without life. Kuznetsov Street, like all the Soviet avenues built for a limitless future, was ten lanes wide, and though never free from a moderate stream of trucks night and day, there was about it an inhuman desolation: it was a street of wheels, empty of men. And beyond the river, the only vertical piercing this horizontal monotony was the high steel tower that jams broadcasts from the West. It straddled there like a robot guardian of the people. Even at night, when lights make cities exciting, the view from the Hotel Ukraine was not. It evoked only the consciousness that this was indeed Moscow and that I was in another world inexpressibly distant from my own. I felt shut in, shut out: the chronic climate of this city and state.

Yet the room was a haven of sorts from the Ukraine lobby, a formidable prelude to Russian life, more dismaying even than the first view of the building itself. Moscow's skyscrapers — the University, two hotels, two apartment houses, and two government bureaus — are huge without being heroic, high without being lofty. Palaces of pride, they are frosted with dismal decorative detail in the worst nineteenth-century taste. And yet, in the interior dialogue that, in my isolation, became the only free exchange, a second voice said, "What they aimed for was good: to honor, with great planning and effort, the concepts of government, housing, learning, and hospitality." And when I was taken through the University, this honoring was constantly evident: in the spacious procession of halls and rooms, in their permanent materials, in the care with which they were swept and polished.

But at the Ukraine I encountered two immediate depressants: the dim lighting that makes all public plates in Moscow forlorn and joyless, and a smell that I have never smelt before and find hard to describe. It is a mixture of stale cooking, old clothing, and the exhalations of rooms dusted but never washed. One could not say that the lobby was airless, because the doors to the outside chill were always open and no one took off his overcoat. But what one breathes there is nevertheless not oxygen.

The people in the lobby at the Ukraine prompted my first voice to say, "This is the new capital of the world." Here were all the races from Near East to Far East, from Africa to Siberia, from the Caucasus to China. Here were eggplant-skinned men in caracul caps and pure white linen tunics, coffee-colored men in long camel's-hair nightgowns, Peking Chinese in austere and neutral uniforms, and the ubiquitous satellite hordes in light gray coats and hats and cheap tan shoes that proclaim the new proletarian, technological man. I found myself amused at the leap of kinship that arose in me when I saw the craggy features and easy strides of British delegates (there was an oceanographic conference going on) or heard the gentle Oxford accents issuing from the soft faces of Indians.

As for the hotel staff, they presented my first view of that fatigue which is stamped, it seems, on the face of every Russian over thirty. I have never seen more tired people than the women — most Russian clerks are women — at the administration desks, the Intourist office, and in the elevators. Some of the operators are fairly young and use lipstick or wear beads and high heels. But most are gray with weariness, their ungroomed hair tucked under the eternal kerchief, their shoulders huddled beneath shawls. Weary, too, are the women guardians on each floor, the dispensers of keys, the watchers of aliens, the arbiters of service. But the added dimension of power is inclined to make them hostile: suspicion is their companion, and rarely permits a smile except to their own kind, the maids on the floor. On the streets of Moscow and Leningrad I saw such women multiplied a thousandfold. I had always thought of the Russians as intense and volatile, surging between exuberance and despair, but I have not seen a society so devoid of beauty of the manifestations of joy, so monolithically drab as these people appear to be.

But my second voice would say, "Wait a minute. Your little guide is pretty and gay, isn't she?" And I remembered the handsome young couple at the Marriage Palace in Leningrad, flushed with pleasure and embarrassment: the handsome aging wife of the architect in the same city; the pleasant young woman on the train from Moscow to Leningrad who offered me her food; the warm and eager ex-sailor on the plane back to Moscow, determined to make me understand Russian, pressing small gifts on me.

As for fatigue and drabness, my second voice said, "Why not? Revolution, war, famine, desolation have taken a terrible toll of them, and so has the merciless absence of privacy. For people who live several to a room, sleep is a holiday."

As for the coldness to Americans, the U-2 struck much deeper than we know, reviving fear. The Russians are told, every day and night, how we plot against them. I have heard what they hear.

My second voice also reminded me that I had no access to their private pleasures; somewhere the Russians must smile. Surely the elite musicians and writers and actors and scientists and party bosses in their handsome skyscraper flats laugh and joke and horse around of an evening, and even their poorer comrades — the people you see — must soften with vodka after a day's work.

Perhaps the distractions of beauty, hilarity, or overt sex are permissible only in the context of purpose. A woman can be beautiful to serve the Soviet stage or ballet or cinema; laughter is for the circus; sex is for the Soviet family. But to what end is woman merely beautiful to herself? I looked for feminine consciousness of body, but even the few well-made and well-complexioned young women dressed to deny their breasts and waists and legs and made no effort with their hair. Beauty as a luxury had a low priority.

Yet then I remember a fashion show at the enormous filigreed GUM department store, where pretty women modeled attractively simple clothes in current style. The crowd—the women kerchief-headed, as many old as young—looked at them with a look of transfiguration, as if shown the Holy Grail.

I saw the Soviet people not only during their endless shuffle along the streets, going to and from work, but also in parks constructed for their relaxation, in theaters, in museums, and in exhibitions. Except for ecstatic clapping at a Sviatoslav Richter recital, a general gravity prevailed. Only the children seemed released in laughter during their games or at the wonderful theaters run for them. And here again we have a Soviet pride, their dominant one. They swaddle their children with love and tenderness, and the children—strong and vital and shining—seem to be free of the distractions of doubt and fear. I saw a number of them in a typical day nursery, variously dressed, ebullient. They sang a May Day song like little patriots and they chanted, "What do all people want? Peace! Peace! Peace!" but they also sang "Hicawry dickawry duck, ze mouse rhan up ze cluck," and although they were disciplined and orderly, I was conscious of no repression. Nor did I see a clouded or withdrawn face.

Will they grow like their fathers and mothers? Or is this a new race freed from the crushing burdens of past wars and the rising state? When they inherit the four-day week, the new apartments, and possibly world dominance, will their faces lighten? Or will they also inherit the airless isolation, the rigid compartmentalization that seals up their present?

I had not realized before just how encapsuled and stratified the

Russians were until my own status in their land shed light on this. I came as a tourist, although the word "Writer" followed "Occupation" in my passport and I made no secret of my professional interests. But did this fact help me to meet Soviet writers? No. Had I come under the aegis of the ministry of culture, this could have been arranged, but as a tourist it was difficult if not impossible. Furthermore, what kind of writer did I want to meet? On what subject? When I said it did not matter—journalist, novelist, critic, anything, so long as the writer was willing to talk to me—the shades were pulled down. I had to be specific. All right, I said, I write a lot of television criticism; could I meet a television critic? We have none, they said. Well, could I meet a writer who was interested in the subject of mass communications and their functions? After a week, a highly intelligent editor of a technological magazine for youth was produced and a conversation of reasonable flexibility did ensue. But this entailed maximum effort on the part of the intermediary. I had hoped to see a ballet class, but when they asked "Are you a dancer?" and I said I was not, the issue was closed. I asked to see a certain building. "Are you an architect?" they said. and when I said no, they asked, "Then why are you interested?" The idea of a broad humanistic interest seemed inconceivable.

The more I saw and the more I heard, the more apparent this lack of cross-pollination became. Musicians met musicians, dancers dancers, actors actors, teachers teachers, and editors editors, and only in the highest echelons, it seemed, did they overlap. But how can a culture emerge from this? Where is the generous, general room of ideas on which imagination lives?

By and large, Soviet culture lives off its own fat. Superb as their execution of ballet may be, professionally healthy as their theater productions can be, brilliant as their performing musicians are, the forward movement seems to have come to a halt decades ago. Imagination and vitality still prevail in their marvelous puppet shows, but the word is "still"; they were always superior and unique.

Visual beauty died with the czars; the Kremlin itself, the onion-domed churches, the palaces of Petersburg—for it is Peter's city, given glory by foreigners like Rossi and Rastrelli and Cameron—only these in Soviet Russia enrich the eye and elate the heart. The painting, sculpture, and architecture of the Soviet state are generally atrocious. I thought if I saw another statue of Soviet youth striding forward into the future, arms outraised, I would scream. Everywhere this deadly moralism sucks the life out of contemporary expression. It belongs, in fact, with death: the graves of the party notables and artist-heroes in the Kremlin cemetery are surmounted by marble portraits of the deceased, faithful to the last mole. In heavy cold rain, with the leaves fallen and sodden, more than they had died.

Yet balanced against these present blights, said my other voice, is the enormous care with which the present Russians preserve their past beauties. Millions of rubles and artisan-hours go into restoring the palace at Tsarskoe-Selo (now Pushkin village) from the vicious multilations of the German army: a job of many years and infinite skill and patience, whether in the reconstruction of elaborate inlaid flooring or of the innumerable painted vignettes that adorn walls and ceilings. When work is finished, as in the Ostankino Palace outside Moscow, the result is breathtaking in its elegance; and the shuffling crowds, equipped with the mandatory felt slippers, are awed into silence. They know what they have inherited. And my other voice said surely this past loveliness must in time educate the eye and refine the taste. Perhaps the old, simple people who stand enthralled before the cloying illustrative realism of party painters may not change, but what of the young?

Whatever I saw, wherever I went in Moscow or Leningrad, my interior dialogue persisted, balancing first impact with further thought. I would quail at the bleakness of Moscow's great arteries but admire the Soviets for their generous planning. When I despaired at the constant injection of dogma into the young, I had to remember the faces of schoolchildren at the Theater for Young Spectators in Leningrad, in whose faces I saw a purity and sense of wonder rare in our own young.

The mediocrity and expensiveness of most consumer products was everywhere evident. But so was the profusion of bookshops, and the fact that subway stands were filled not with comics but with inexpensive books on everything from electronics to fairy tales. I remember, too, that on the train from Moscow to Leningrad, every third Russian appeared to be reading a book.

In an atmosphere that seemed to me cold if not hostile, I could not help but notice the kindness of the people to each other and especially to their children. Only in queues—their daily, hourly penance—did they explode into truculence, and I could not blame them.

The relentless bleakness of their new housing repelled me, but I had to remember that they paid a minimal rent, not only for their premises but for a system that included a nursery, a clinic, a well-equipped playground, workshops, and sometimes a theater in each block unit.

I have mentioned their compartmentalization, but there is something to be said for providing spacious quarters (usually the palaces of former nobles) where scientists, teachers, doctors, architects, and farmers can meet their own kind after hours. It is all part of this pattern of pride in profession which, precisely because it is collective rather than personal, sustains the Soviet citizen. It is their "togetherness." Like ours, too, it can mean an abdication of responsibility.

There are, no doubt, delinquents in Russia. I saw a number of furtive adolescents who bore little resemblance to the heroic figures of Soviet youth breasting the future. But the Soviets manage to keep most of their young off the streets and busy, not only in school hours but in the many "circles" provided by the labor or professional units to which their elders belong. Thus the son of an auto worker can go to the local auto circle after school and find there the room and equipment for any hobby that may attract him, from ship-model building to acrobatics. I find it sad that "aimless play" is discouraged, but an equal case could be made against the aimless entertainment of our own spare time.

To anyone who has free access to many (and contradictory) truths, the Soviet enclosure provokes frustration and incredulity. Every day, in print, on radio, on television, the facts are withheld or tailored to their straitjacket needs. During the U.N. weeks of explosion, Krushchev won victory after victory. Neither word nor camera betrayed the slightest setback. The Soviet people, presented hourly with the tumultuous applause of the Communist bloc, were spared all evidence that a great part of the world, neutral as well as Western-oriented, was shocked and alarmed by their chairman's attempt to wreck the United Nations. Castro was, of course, lionized as freedom's champion. Imperialism, colonialism, aggression — daily the tired, inapplicable slogans paraded the pages and the airwaves. I said some of this, in modified terms to a Soviet writer and broadcaster. "It is true," he said, "that we still have too much dogma. It is a leftover from the war, and it will decrease as time goes on."

They say, of course; that we have our own dogma: a blanket hatred and fear of Communism that makes any recognition of its achievements politically and morally impermissible. Communication, certainly, was not made easier by the many American tourists who preferred to expound the superiorities of our way of life rather than listen to the accomplishments of theirs. "They are not," said one weary American official, "doing us much good."

Certainly, too, three weeks is no time to judge a society kept aloof not only by an isolation officially imposed and a distrust genuinely felt but a language unshared. What I have written here is merely a chronicle of reactions, immediately felt and then deliberately examined. And if I were left, after a period of turmoil and questioning, with anything approaching a large conclusion, it would again have two voices.

I believe that the Soviet people are on an ascending graph and that they know it: the climate of confidence in Soviet destiny is palpable, as is the will and capacity to pay for it. They know that they could not have afforded the democratic luxury of choice.

Yet I cannot believe that this degree of enclosure can be forever sustained. Too many Russians must be too intelligent to nourish themselves indefinitely on the synthetic food of dogma, too talented to find in technology their only expression. I have the feeling that there is in many, and will be in many more, an unquenchable desire to see the world whole and to walk freely among others. A direct and meeting gaze in the eyes of some Russians gave me, the feeling that within them, too, a constant dialogue goes on. But their second voice was inaudible.

JFK:
The Beginning

What did you miss if you watched President Kennedy's inauguration on television, instead of being there to see it "live"?

Obviously, you missed a cold so severe that distinguished statesmen wrapped mufflers around their chins and under their hats. It was so bitter that the crowds at the Capitol kept up a steady drumming with their feet, a low thunder, to keep them from freezing. But you missed, too, an exhilaration produced by many things: by the piercing blue sky above the glittering white Capitol, by the snapping ripple of flags, by the strong tension between the thousands looking and the object looked at, the young man with the thick hair and no overcoat.

What else did you miss in your warm rooms? Little things; the voice of an announcer coming out of the portable radio two seats away saying, "This is a colorful crowd," and one of the onlookers saying "yeah — red noses, yellow eyeballs, and blue hands."

And did you, when you watched Marian Anderson sing "The Star Spangled Banner" on television, notice the wife of some dignitary to her right? Smartly furred, she used the national anthem to adjust her hat and skirt and stockings and then to look for something evidently missing. She found it just as Miss Anderson sang what I must now remember as '...and the bag was still there!"

Perhaps you felt the same as we did when John F. Kennedy gave his inaugural address. But I wonder, for how can public yearning and growing elation be transmitted on the screen?

What did we share, you on television and we at the scene? We both saw the grace of Mr. Eisenhower, the overabundance of Kennedy women with all that hair, teeth, and energy, the bounce of HST, the dignity of the Supreme Court Justices. And we must have dwelt long on the face of the President's young wife, not only because of its beauty but because of a touching inwardness, a quality of serene removal that reminded me of archaic Greek or Khmer heads: a smile that had nothing public about it, that spoke of things withheld and guarded.

We may have shared, I think, an exasperation with the churchmen, particularly with Cardinal Cushing, whose rasping pontifications brought neither light nor beauty nor meaning to this event. He had a great, a singular, a wonderful chance to help all Americans celebrate, in their first Catholic President, their liberation from prejudice, and all he could conjure up was hell's fire from the lectern. Only the Greek Orthodox invocation drew any approval.

As for the parade, you viewers, I am sure, lost nothing but the brotherhood of cold and the long walk from the Capitol to the reviewing stands; one way, indeed, of restoring circulation in icy feet. You probably saw the President's stand and its occupants much better than we did, and the expressions on the faces of the high officials as they drove in their open cars. But if you noticed the deputy marshal of the parade, William Walton, you may not have shared my affectionate amusement at seeing a painter, writer, and friend, in that exalted position, and watching him doff his silk hat from his prizefighter's head with all the elegance of an old political hand. It was a big day for the arts.

It was not a big day for Robert Kennedy's public relations: from where I sat, his perch on the back of his car was viewed with distaste. The new Attorney General was not, after all, on a float, nor riding a buffalo.

THE LONG VIGIL

There are moments of such magnitude that they must be clearly remembered. And it might serve a purpose to record what one American, and surely multitudes more, saw and felt and thought sitting before the television set from Friday to Monday, November 22-25, 1963.

This was not viewing. This was total involvement.

I was out when the President was shot and saw only the replayed tape, first of him waving and smiling to cheering Dallas faces, and then the wild, careering moment of the murder: the insane kaleidoscope in the camera's eye as it swung and jolted from a photographer running through chaos to commotion. From then on, with few intervals away, I stayed before the set, knowing that I must give myself over entirely to an appallingly tragedy, and that to evade it was a treason of the spirit.

It is hard to remember the exact sequence of events that Friday; incredulity and shock at this immense unreason left no place for an orderly succession in the mind. It was all ambulances, police cars, corridors, bewildered newsmen, and once in a while the small figure of the President's wife, briefly recognized and then eclipsed.

There was a glaring tawdriness about everything in Dallas that day: from the fat police to the sleek ambulance, from the warehouse walls with those terrible open windows to the thruway that led to the hospital.

Later there was the scene in the plane when a woman judge swore in the big man with the scored face as President of the United States, as Mrs. Johnson and Mrs. Kennedy stood by. You tried to take it in, to find solace in the orderly, quiet succession, but it was too much to take. Through those hours you saw the face of Lee Oswald, thin and pasty and small-mouthed, and you thought what a miserable worm he was and how even hate for him was overwhelmed by horror of his act. And then when you heard them say he was a Marxist you thought, "Oh, God, it is bad enough without this. Here we go — from now on the old hysteria has fuel to burn on again." And you thought of the smugness and relief of the right-wingers and the wise shaking of many heads over leftist subversives, and what this would do to us in the time to come.

It was only later, much later, when the plane that carried the President's body and the President's wife and their successors arrived at Andrews Air Force Base, that the implacable sequence began.

I sat there watching men struggling through the door of the plane's hydraulic lift with the casket and I thought, there he is, and I thought of that shattered head underneath and the high shoulders and long legs, and of how he had looked when he walked into press conferences with a quick step and his thick-haired head slightly bent forward and his down-slanted eyes slightly quizzical. And I watched Mrs. Kennedy being helped down to the ground by two men and follow the casket to the ambulance with her brother-in-law.

As for us, the millions, we could not take our eyes from that metal box. It was not morbidity, it was a desperate attachment, a holding on to what was already lost until there was not even this rectangle and remnant to cling to. I followed it every inch of the way, I watched each time the nine proud young men carried it up the steps and into the White House, and then on to the caisson, to the Capitol, to the cathedral, and to the grave. I imagined them telling of this until the day they died, and what it felt like to know his body was in their hands.

The simplicity of that box with the flag on it, the great loneliness of the executive in death as in life, were made just bearable by the sturdy gray horses, nuzzling and jerking against their traces, by the beautifully ridden lead horse with his high head and rhythmic gait, by the fretting and rearing riderless black horse behind, by the single sailor with the President's flag. I was grateful every inch of the way for these traditions, for the awful solemnity of the muffled drums; I was proud of the silence they beat in and the grief they echoed.

And I, like millions, was immeasurably proud of the President's wife. Nothing will ever erase from my mind the sight of that small, erect black figure on the steps of the Capitol with her small children holding her hands. Her control, grace, and dignity were miracles, demanding from us who watched a restraint which we could not always match. Every moment she made was right, and hard to bear.

Hour after hour, wherever the President lay, I watched the people who came to honor him. The familiar faces of senators and judges, of Cabinet members, of the family itself were made less familiar by their shock and strain. Most of them looked years older.

And during all this, the shuffle of feet, the tolling of bells, the beating of drums, the clopping of horses' hooves, the click of the honor guard's rifles, the shrilling of whistles, for four interminable days I listened to the familiar interpreters of events: Edward P. Morgan and Howard K. Smith, Walter Cronkite and Eric Sevareid and Charles Collingwood, Chet Huntley and David Brinkley, Marvin Kalb and Robert Pierpont and so many more who never failed us or history. Shaken as they visibly were, infinitely weary as they became, they maintained calm and reason and insight through the marathon of mourning.

The madness punctuated the mourning, as millions watched, that Sunday in Dallas. I could not believe what I saw. The clutter of newsmen and their microphones in that basement corridor, the milling and the talking, and then those big fat men bringing the prisoner, suddenly the back of a man with a hat, and then Oswald doubled, and then pandemonium, scuffles, shouts, and young Tom Truitt and his microphone in and out of the picture trying to find out what happened. Questions seethed through my mind: how in God's name could the police expose a President's alleged assassin to the jumble of people at that close range? How could anyone with a gun get right to him? What kind of law is this in Dallas? Who on earth did it? Why?

And then as we heard some of the answers, incredulity was supplanted by digust and fury, and these in turn by a sense of the insanely grotesque: a striptease proprietor, a small-time crook, had deprived the American people and the accused murderer of their President of justice on the actual premises of law: police headquarters. Then outrage took over again: outrage at the enormity of the act, at violence so close to the surface, at the boundless bungling of those fat Texas police. It was in relief that we came back to the President's body and the muffled drums. Sorrow, however vast, was better than outrage. That could wait till later.

By Monday, I had watched the leaders of the nations of the world arrive the night before at Dulles Airport as a drawn Dean Rusk, waiting and pacing, greeted each in turn. Now I watched them assemble at the White House for that walk to the Cathedral of St. Matthew. They gathered behind the President's wife and two brothers, once more back of the caisson with the President's body, fretting Blackjack and the seven gray horses. You could see her features under the heavy black veil only enough to know that they were still composed; her arms hung straight at her sides. Robert Kennedy's face bore, as always during the four long days, the bleakness of devastation together with, it seemed to me, a mighty anger.

Slowly the cortege and the leaders of the nations walked in the winter sun to the cathedral, and then we, all of us again, were in the church. Millions, I am sure, were deeply moved by what transpired there. Unhappily I felt Cardinal Cushing not as an assuager of my grief, but as an intruder into it: the grating cadences of his loud voice, the harshness of his Latin and English speech, took from the service much that would have been beautiful. I told myself that this old man was a lifelong friend of the President and his family, that if they loved him there was much to love, and that his sorrow was boundless. But I wanted his talking to end in the church as I wanted it to end later at Arlington, and as, so few years ago, I wanted it to come to an end at the inauguration of the man he now mourned. The silence was the balm.

In Arlington we heard the skirl of bagpipes, as we walked close to the grave, we watched the honor guard take the flag from the casket and hold it taut between them, we saw the standing mourners still as stone. Then we saw the flag folded over and over and placed in the hands of Jacqueline Kennedy. And with tears now uncontainable, we heard the high and lonely bugle notes of taps.

The light had gone out; the lights were lit; not only on the grave of the murdered President but in the halls of state where the new President, only hours later, received the leaders with whom, from this moment on, he would have to treat.

Only this scene, a sort of social sarabande unreal in its conventionality, could have finally stemmed our tears. Here was the big new President pumping hand after hand, smiling and nodding; here were, except for Charles de Gaulle, much smaller men trying to impress themselves on the mind of the new executive; here were old allies and old adversaries, and the new men of new countries, coming to pay court in the hopes of being courted, anxious to tell their people what this new leader was like; how he looked and talked, how he behaved to them.

And then, finally, there were the lights in the private apartments of the White House; and when we saw these we turned the set off and left Mrs. John F. Kennedy to the protective darkness, and ourselves — the millions and millions of us — to a respite denied her.

ON
NEW YORK

This city is full of fragmented people, from those who talk to themselves and move jerkily to those whose faces are set in hostility or negation.

There are many others, I know, who do not feel this. They are the very successful who can afford to cushion themselves with money against the myriad discomforts of our streets, who are chauffeur-driven to work, who pay dearly to be served in grand restaurants and see plays from the best seats, who live high above the tumult, who can save their energies for the exhilaration of fighting on the highest levels of their profession.

There are those, too, who have never known New York as it used to be, and who find it so far superior to the cities and towns of their birth and childhood that they accept it without reservation. And there are those who, never having lived in London or Paris or Rome, do not know what civilized living in a city can be.

For the young on their way up, New York is still the sum of their dreams. For the tourist, it is the greatest show on earth. And for the educated foreigner, it is often an intoxification of freedom, a kaleidoscope of those shifting delights, of anonymity and discovery, which the traditional pattern of life at home does not permit him.

The unceasing ferment of this town is creative as well as destructive. If the talent of America is not born here, it usually flowers here, for this is the stimulus, the forcing ground, and the marketplace.

And people care. There are citizens bent on the salvage of the young and lost, the sick and lonely, the alien and the old, and the decent many who cannot live in the city of their choice if they must choose between luxury, which they cannot afford, and squalor.

Without such efforts, New York may become a place to shun, a giant trap inviting its own destruction. Until either future, this New Yorker has set down one image of the city, deeply held: an atmosphere of potential. Above the towers, the ceiling is unlimited.

While I am strong and productive, there is no other city I could accept as my home without a sense of exile.

ENVOI

I believe in the immortality of rooms. Although it was torn down fifty years ago and more, I can still walk through the apartment of my youth on Amsterdam Avenue and see every single thing in it, suspended in the air, forever held intact through time. One corner of it, seven floors high, looking south on Amsterdam and west to Broadway, is like the bridge of a ship. There on a window seat, with the grand piano behind me and the Louvre *Victory* on a pedestal to the left, I looked every evening around six to see my father come out of the subway three blocks away and walk home. All day he taught violin at his settlement school on Third Street, and we — my mother often watched for him with me — would know by his walk what the day had done to him. The thin, tall, graceful figure would either stride those blocks lightly or plod them slowly; his head held high or his shoulders stooped. The moment he neared our corner, our white Persian cat (who was not looking) would bound to the front door and wait there until he opened it.

Still there, suspended, is the dining room full of golden oak, the only remembered lapse in taste, where we ate, argued, and studied at night, my brother Leopold at calculus while I was subtracting, or at Ovid while I was at Thackeray. There, swinging between the folding doors of my passage-bedroom, is the trapeze where I hung. There, at the end of the long, dark hall, is the room of my brother, where a sort of pantry exhaled the results of chemical experiment. There, on the other side of this rambling place, is the adult sanctuary of my parents, a small room (inviolable) full of photographs of musicians, signed affectionately. The apartment is full of music: Brahms, Beethoven, and Mozart sonatas halted by arguments in rising voices or played in the serenity of union; Schumann and Rachmaninoff practiced by my brother, my own erratic fumbling at the keys; a trio, a quartet, a quintet with visitors. The air on the seventh floor on Amsterdam Avenue still rings.

VIE DE BOHÉME

I don't know just how I discovered Greenwich Village somewhere in the twenties, but I suspect I posed for an artist who lived there. I had the sort of face that enthralled painters and discouraged boys, and I know that from fifteen on I spent much of my time standing, sitting, and lying in studios while men paced back and forth, squinted, laid on pigment or pushed clay, and talked of bone structure, themselves, and me. And since most of them worked and lived in the Village, I began to know the streets and the life and the studios quite well.

Not only did Greenwich Village have the savor of the Europe I loved from early childhood; it stood for a kind of rebellion against the lives of musicians I was beginning to find too respectable. I knew my parents were artists, but they were very moral, too; and the atmosphere of hard work, regular meals, and *gemütlichkeit* was beginning to bear rather heavily on a girl steeped in bad as well as good romantic literature, and determined to live dangerously at whatever cost. A studio was obviously the place to do it in, and I already saw myself as a modern Maja Desnuda or Madame X on the walls of the Metropolitan, driving men with desire.

It was with some surprise, therefore, and suppressed chagrin that I found the studio little more sinful than the music room, and the artist, by and large, just as serious. What happened in Greenwich Village was not the toppling of virtue so much as the expansion of vision. I began to see things I had never seen before; not only objects but a way of looking at them, not only shapes but a way of feeling them. My ears had been open to sound since birth, and the structure of music had entered my being. Yet musicians are less aware, I think, than all other creative people, of the specific pleasures of the eye. The homes of most of the virtuosi, conductors, singers, and composers I knew in youth were densely cluttered, curtained and tasseled, and suffused with the green of potted ferns. I could never understand how they could manage to divorce the beauty of sound from the beauty of sight, but they did. They were quite happy in their airless nests.

The bareness of the studio, then, came as a revelation. In this white purity, lit evenly and coldly by skylights, every object in the room had meaning. In Greenwich Village I first saw animal skulls, bleached; empty bottles chosen for their shape; artifacts from Mexico or New Mexico; fruit in huge bowls; woven cloths of strong colors from exotic places; plain wood tables, unvarnished; windows without curtains; pillows on floors; and studio couches.

In Greenwich Village I first saw artists' wives. They all wore bangs, were inclined to fleshiness, and dressed in full skirts and peasant blouses when the fashion was knee-length sheaths. Instead of single long strands of pearls, they wore hammered silver and turquoise matrix. Even more remarkable, they could cook fragrant spaghetti and exotic stews. Uptown, German, Irish, or Finnish cooks made solid meals that were heavy with potatoes and dumplings.

In Greenwich Village I first heard people speak of breasts and thighs and buttocks and bellies as one would speak of mountains, rivers, bread, and fruit; and I first discovered that it was possible to look at a naked body impersonally, as form, texture, and substance.

In Greenwich Village I first heard sex talked of with joy and amusement, as an open delight and not a secret urge. If all these revelations sound unimaginably naïve to a generation drilled in four-letter words and the techniques of intercourse, I can only say that people like my parents were not only inhibited but fastidious, and found much ugly that is now routine for us. In consequence, my pose as *femme fatale,* borrowed heavily from the bookshelves, concealed a staggering innocence. Greenwich Village, in the animal simplicity that resides in most painters, played a large part in dissipating it, without shock or squalor.

CENTRAL PARK

Central Park is many things. It is the calm eye in the center of a hurricane. It is the vision of men who knew man's needs. It is the measure of seasons in a city which tries to insulate itself from them. It is the refuge of wild things escaping stone. It is a zone of danger. It is the only sleeping land in a sleepless city. And it is the only place, aside from the Jersey and Brooklyn shores and the Upper Bay, from which the dream of Manhattan is wholly visible because the eye has room to embrace it and the heart the distance to love it.

Central Park is also the view from my window; standing close, that is. For lying on my bed I see only a wide pane of sky crossed intermittently by the plunge of pigeons, or much farther off and much higher, by the slow, supremely easy arc of gulls as they ride on thermal currents.

Directly below my window is the bridle path, and beyond that a triangle of trees and grass where the neighborhood dogs run free, and beyond that the pompous stone back of Daniel Webster, one of the strange assortment of statues, Shakespeare, Morse, Humboldt, Mazzini, which nobody looks at. But the focal point of the view is the double lake: two winding irregular ponds, the narrow waist between them spanned by a delicate iron bridge, gently arched and persistently Japanese in feeling.

Beyond the lake and its boathouse, the Metropolitan Museum to the northeast and the bandstand shell to the southeast, are the apartments of Fifth Avenue transformed not by distance so much as by light. For when a clear sun sets in early fall and winter they are washed in an apricot glow, their windows inflamed and brilliant, and then they might be some desert city of palaces. So beautiful are they, behind dark trees and against a darkening sky, I am impelled to rush home and stare at them before the sun is down and the grayness takes over.

And if I crane my neck and face south from the Dakota, I see even greater splendor: the cluster of stalagmites south of Fifty-Ninth Street, a pattern of older spires and newer slabs so magnificent in their soaring arrangement that the accident which is Manhattan seems a deliberate creative act.

When is the Park most beautiful from my window? In heavy snow, I think; or the pale green fuzzing of early spring. When the snow has stopped falling and is still blindingly white, and the lake is frozen, the rough ice sparsely dotted with skating and slipping black figures, and the branches are black, then Breughel comes alive. And all the dogs, leaping and racing black silhouettes, are delirious in the snow. Later, after the interminable dead brown sleep of winter, after snow, the first faint blurring of the trees is an excitement. And still later, when the lake is alive with colored boats and rowing people, distance again bestows an innocence on this popular pleasure which closer attention might dispel: the rowdies shout four-letter words as they ram a stranger, and fat men with cigars throw bottles in the lake.

There is a certain lushness about full summer; the heavy denseness of green over all, the leaves unstirred by wind, the whole Park breathing like a tired beast in the intolerable heat of July. But summer stirs the beast, too, for this is the time of danger when human animals hide in the cover of leaves and darkness. And even from my room, high above, I can hear on a stifling night cries which might be horseplay but which could also be screams of fear. Indeed, I once heard a woman cry "Help! Help!" and I rushed to the window at midnight, but saw nothing except the lamplight shining through the heavy trees and the rest in blackness.

I don't know how much the eye of a child has changed since I was small (I suspect that a profusion of secondhand marvels has reduced the capacity for delight in firsthand ones), but to the very young, the granite boulders in the Park must still be peaks for conquering, and a thicket of firs an ambush beckoning courage. Certainly, where I was scaling these slabs, today's children have sculpture: Hans Christian Andersen and his duck, or the too-elaborate Alice in Wonderland tea party. And where I clung proudly to my wooden carousel horse, feeling (I know now) that wonderful sense of pride which a real horse gives his rider, the kids are now gliding up and down on theirs with the same proud glee in their eyes.

Skating, too, is a different matter. Then there was no Wollman rink, and we skated only on the lakes when they froze over. Rough or smooth, they offered all of the space in the world and no need for Muzak. No need to go round and round in one direction, no confinement of the experts to one small circle. In the long fingers and coves of the lakes each could take his pace and attempt his curves without the risk of collision. This was a great freedom of the Park in winter, a resort five blocks from my family's building.

I do not remember the Park zoo as a child; we went to the Bronx for our animals. Later, much later, I took my own child to the little zoo by the Arsenal, as most mothers do. But my real pleasure in it is part of a present ritual as a stroller. A long watch at the sea lion's pool is imperative. There is a large one, who looks male, and two smaller ones, who look female; these two have something clinging and tender about them as they suffer his ill temper. Often I have seen one of them rub up against his fat and shining flank only to get an irritable shrug, a sharp bark in the face, and an edging away. I watch them as they stretch and doze when their bellies are full, and I watch them in their ludicrous anxiety for the midday fish: a constant craning of necks toward the keeper's expected approach, a leaping out of water and peering through the railings, blowing a fishy breath, barking and bristling. But I love them best when they are simply playing: performing an underwater ballet so swift and graceful and full of humor (they race below belly upward, their flippers folded over, then shoot out of the water with silly bravura faces) that no sense of captivity remains. They are the only animals there that do not make me actively sad. I cannot bear to look at the big cats, lions, tigers, leopards, cheetahs, because of their hopeless constriction, forced either to doze with their beautiful yellow eyes open or to pace in padded silence all day long. Nor can I find any amusement, as I used to, in the big apes. The look in the eyes of the gorilla frightens me; it is full of an implacable hatred.

There is a yak there, too, from whom I must turn away. He has a distorted horn that curves up under his chin and he must know his distortion, for he usually stands in a dark corner of his cell, a big black shaggy heap of depression. And I am embarrassed for the molting camel.

But the Barbary wild sheep fascinate me. They stand in absolute stillness on small rocks to which their hooves seem fastened, while their big goat eyes, full of amber interior light, see nothing. And when there is a baby llama or a baby Sika deer or tahr, I am enchanted by their tentative necks, their long lashes, and their feeble legs, so easily buckled. Theirs is a vulnerability which even our smallest Park children seem to lack.

For I watch their faces too, as they come, singly with parents, or in long queues with teachers, to look at the animals, and there is a toughness in too many of them. Their amusement at the animals is contemptuous, and I keep wondering whether anybody has given them a sense of reverence for the multiple marvels of species, for the separate identities of these beasts. Pity, certainly, is an alien emotion to the young. But what of wonder?

The real lovers of the zoo by the Arsenal appear to be foreigners. In fact, it is the foreigners who walk in any weather, finding in the Park some answer to their craving for peace in a city that provides no islands of rest or simple sociability in its midst.

It is a source of amazement to me that the Park is so little used by the people of the city, except as an escape from heat in summer. For nine months of the year it is virtually empty during the day, except for the playgrounds and playing fields, and on holidays. On glorious days of sun and wind or of soft grayness I have crossed the Park time and again and met no more than five others on the way, if I stayed off the jogging routes. It is this very loneliness now that makes me walk by the main arteries rather than on the smaller paths; even in daylight I cannot rule out the thought of danger.

There is special pleasure in watching squirrels. Their tails fold so neatly over their backs, their paws are so expert holding nuts. Do they remember where they buried their own nuts, or do they dig up somebody else's? I cannot see one of these respectable rodents without remembering a fire last year that burned out a hollow tree on the edge of the Park. Firemen came to extinguish the blaze, and when an elderly woman passing by asked one of the hosemen, "What is it, officer, what happened?" he turned to her with a face empty of guile and said, "Squirrel — smoked in bed."

And what of the birds? Early on a spring morning I have looked out of my window and seen a little band of people across the lake, their elbows raised as they hold binoculars up. They are bird watchers, of course, and a happier company never was, for they live on hope interspersed with shocks of joy: there he is, the first hermit thrush!, or the first rose-breasted grosbeak!, or the first magnolia warbler! After an hours of this they can go to their offices with a sense of buoyant completion denied their fellows. I am neither knowledge-able nor dedicated enough to be of their kind, but even I find joy in the flight of strange birds and a call I never heard before, a solace in the midst of gigantic artifice.

Still another dedicated group are the model-boat sailors on the round pond at Seventy-Second Street. Their miniature yachts, perfect with mahogany and brass, intricate rigging, and their bright pennants, are products of great love and years of hours. And when they take the wind, lean over and race toward the other lip of the pool leaving a miniature hissing wake, their owners are no less solicitous than parents would be.

In summer, music and drama will bring people to the Park. Although spoiled like most New Yorkers by a wealth of both on easier terms, and averse to crowds, I have gone on a suffocating night to look and hear. The reward is less in the performances than in the faces of those who listen. The old seem less tired, and the young, in attitudes of love on the grass, more tender.

But on the fringes of the innocent, the evil gather. Heat and night bring the roaches from their crevices, and then the Park becomes a jungle. Even in my childhood, there was danger: our doctor arrived one evening bruised and cut from an assault by two thugs who took his watch and money. And in broad daylight, two things happened which I cannot forget. Once a man with his features obliterated by blood came out of a thicket, staggering, and I fled in terror. And once, in deep winter, in the same rambles which the prudent now avoid, I came upon a man in an act which I did not understand but which wholly revolted me. I ran, sickened, the half mile to my home.

Now, of course, there is more violence. The Park has become not only a stalking ground for young predators and rapists; it is a point of assignation. I need go no further than my window to see the figure of a man waiting behind a tree, joined later by another man, who walks with him under the heavy shadows of leaves and out of sight.

Frederick Law Olmsted and Calvert Vaux, who created Central Park from a tract of featureless land spotted with shanties, had the backing of a mayor, Ambrose C. Kingsland, who furthered their aim, and a board of commissioners distinguished by the presence of William Cullen Bryant, who edited the New York *Evening Post* from 1829 to 1878, and Andrew Jackson Downing, who edited the *Horti-culturist*. For five years these men and others fought for this central site, and for five and one-half million dollars it was finally bought from private owners by the city. A triumph over the "practical" rapacity of realtors who wept at the waste of building sites, Central Park became the first park in the United States, and a model for most that followed.

But now Vaux, Olmsted, Kingsland, Bryant and Downing would weep at the Park they made, not if they looked at it from my window, but if they walked its paths as I do and looked closely. Everywhere they would see the litter of cellophane and bottletops in the bottom of every grove, paper cups and cans at the fringes of once-clear lakes, and newspapers left lying on the grass to blow, get sodden, and stick among the twigs.

Some of this, in the middle of a great city, is inescapable. But most of the fault lies with the people for whom the Park was made, many of whom vent on nature what they cannot on stone.

And yet, nothing can spoil the wide sweep of the Sheep Meadow before the great southern towers of Manhattan. Nothing can spoil the brilliant rippled rectangle of the Reservoir. Nothing can spoil what you see when you look from a window on the southern border of the Park: miles and miles of trees and clearings which seem to lead to freedom.

THE RAID
ON CASTALIA
(APRIL 16, 1966)

I was asleep when the police came to Castalia. At least, I had gone to bed before eleven and was aware only at a dim level of consciousness of a great deal of noise and movement around the sixty-two-room house where Dr. Timothy Leary lived. The noise was quite different from the sounds I heard from his room above when I first fell asleep: music with a regular cadence, and the occasional shuffling of feet, I assumed that this noise was merely late party-making by the twenty-four other people spending the night there, and I remember thinking it must be very late and wishing they could be more considerate.

At some point I was conscious that the woman who shared my room had gone to the door to find out what was going on. She came back shortly and said, "The police are raiding us. They want to search us."

I got out of bed and started to put on my raincoat over my improvised nightwear of shorts and a sweater, but she said, "No, they want us to strip." A policewoman with a pleasant face who wore a red suit and carried a shoulder bag came in and we stood there naked while she looked at the inside of our arms and thighs for needle marks.

"I'm just a middle-aged square," I told her. She smiled and said, "so am I, dear," apologized for bothering us, and went out of the room. We learned later that while all the men's belongings were ransacked, only the women were stripped.

We slung on pants and tops and went out on the landing where most of the others were sitting or standing while state troopers and plainclothesmen passed back and forth, searching the maze of rooms for whatever they could find. Occasionally they would return with a paper box, a plant, or a package and take them downstairs. Once someone asked what was in a box, and the trooper said "Goodies!"

Leary was among us, in the jeans and light blue shirt he had worn all day, his bare feet dirty from hours spent chopping down thickets and small trees in a fir grove back of the house.

"I was told they'd be around sometime," he said, "and I've cleared everything out of the house. Anyway, if I were hiding anything, it would be in a place they couldn't find."

His sixteen-year-old son Jack sat on the landing near him with a sullen look on his handsome face. Sometimes he strummed a guitar or banjo. He was joined from time to time by a young man who improvised with him on his own guitar.

During the four hours on the landing of the main stairwell, guarded above and below by plainclothesmen and other troopers, seated or coming and going, we talked and drank cheap red wine from a gallon Leary brought up from the pantry or tea brought by others. We talked and waited and speculated and sometimes joked, but nobody thought it was funny.

It was nearly four in the morning before the police searched my room. In their haste to get through the sliding door they pushed me against a painting on the wall back of me. It fell with a resounding crash and knocked over the wine jug, which somehow on its downward hurtle nicked the upper lip of a young woman standing near me. Blood started to pour from under her nose, while dark wine stains spread on the green mat at our feet. She was taken to the bathroom and mopped up, and returned holding a wad of Kleenex to her mouth.

People were then taken downstairs one at a time for questioning. This intelligent and gentle young woman, who looked much younger than her twenty-eight years, was asked among other things, "Have you had sexual intercourse here?" She said no, she hadn't, and told us later that she wondered what that had to do with anything anyway. Searching through her effects, they took her Vitamin A tablets, her Bufferin, and her prescription diarrhea pills.

The police took down our names and addresses, but asked me only whether I was the one "that knocked down the picture." I said yes, it had fallen down when I was shoved against the wall. Why this should be the only clue of identity of interest to the law mystified me.

At about four-thirty we were all summoned downstairs and told to wait outside the living room. There Leary, mustering a smile, addressed us: "I have an announcement to make. We are in the hands of the Chinese and the Russians. But we have our own agents working, too!" There was scattered and rather forced laughter.

Then we were told to congregate in the living room, where we sat on the mattresses and faced about twelve of the agents of the law at the far end of the room. One of them said, "Those of you whose names I will call off can leave the room."

A young girl who had seemed terrified all through the raid turned to me and whispered, "Then we're not criminals, are we? Does that mean we're innocent — we can go free?"

I said yes, not to worry. They called out all the names except those of Dr. Leary, a mystic from California and his wife, and a young New York photographer.

The rest of us left the room and most of us went to bed. Those who didn't waited to see Leary and the others handcuffed and driven away. Some followed them to the Poughkeepsie jail, to get a last look at the former Harvard professor.

The long night was preceded by a long day. Assigned by a magazine to interview Leary's eighteen-year-old daughter Susan, I had been driven from New York to Millbrook by the public-relations expert in charge of the Timothy Leary Defense Fund and the woman who is his partner. On the way up he briefed me on a number of aspects of the Leary case, speaking factually and knowledgeably, but with obvious affection and admiration for the embattled and legally embroiled proponent of LSD. His only critical observation was that Leary might be a little naïve: "A good man and a brilliant man, but not always realistic in his dealing with the world at large."

There was certainly nothing worldly about the place where Timothy Leary has lived for the last three years. Castalia, named for the foundation that supports his work, consists of several hundred acres of beautiful Dutchess County land once owned by a German named Dietrich, who not only imposed on it the most formal gardens, vistas, chalets, follies, fountains, and fir groves, but also imported two hundred Italians to build him a lodge, a summer-house, and a portcullis entrance knobbled with native gray boulders. He also employed an architect to erect a huge wooden mansion of unparalleled ugliness—the nadir in turrets, porches, and fretted woodwork—as his own main residence. Here Dr. Leary lives, works, and on weekends receives a steady stream of visitors—students, disciples, observers, friends, and curious strangers. The doors are always open.

We arrived about ten-thirty on the morning of Saturday, April 16, driving to the back of the house and finally finding an entrance from the curving front porch. On the right of a bare entrance hall was what seemed to be the living room. I saw mattresses on the floor, on one of which lay a young man, on another a huge Great Dane. To the left was another bare living room, without mattresses but with a Victorian sofa on which were two large paper kites and a pith helmet with yellow ostrich feathers on it. Stuck on the newel post of the massive oak staircase was a stuffed tiger head with a large pink flower in its mouth.

The rooms—every part of the vast house—had the abandoned look of minimal, sporadic care: dusty, empty, disordered, totally depersonalized. As I later saw, nearly all the weekend visitors take a hand in sweeping, tidying, dishwashing, vacuuming, or cooking, but the ceaseless tide of human traffic defies order and cleanliness. The garbage bags are always full, the sink piled with dishes to be washed later, the floors tracked with outside dust, the closets bursting with cartons and junk, the icebox crammed with food.

The kitchen is the main core of the house, and I never saw it, at any time of the day or night, with out at least five people sitting on pads and cushions around a foot-high round wooden table, eating. Breakfast, lunch, and dinner merged imperceptibly, and there was always someone to fry bacon, boil water, make biscuits, mix salad, or prepare the main dish — on this Saturday night a splendidly seasoned fish with all the trimmings.

Who were all these people? Well, on this weekend of the raid, there were twenty-six of us, including Dr. Leary and his son, but not including the two teenagers and five little children belonging to three sets of visiting parents. The older ones were usually outdoors, jumping on the trampoline or exploring the woods or bicycling. But the toddlers — bright eyed, fresh-skinned, and affectionate — were around us all day long, usually in the kitchen, all of them living together in perfect peace and amity.

This was indeed the prevailing climate of this communal household. Apart from the five or six "irregulars" like myself, most of the group at Castalia shared the qualities of affectionate calm, of above-average sensitivity and intelligence, and of mutual helpfulness. The loves of parents for child, of husband for wife, of most of them for Leary, were open and palpable. Only three of the visitors that weekend — all young and male — looked beatnik or withdrawn. Indeed, they withdrew, most of the time, into the woods or their own rooms.

Among the others were the fair and fragile young wife of a well-known bandleader (and mother of five), a young secretary and volunteer worker from Washington, a research psychiatrist working on a Federal grant, a documentary-film photographer, another photographer specializing in Polaroid research, two artist-designers, a dry-goods manufacturer, and a fashion editor on a national magazine for young women.

Most of the men and women at Castalia that weekend had, of course, taken LSD a number of times, and I overheard one of them — the young father with the pure and gentle face — describe to a non-user what he had felt on his last "trip."

"It was so beautiful," he said. "I pushed back time and I pushed back space, and everything was filled with love. You are a part of this great love, part of everything. It was really a transfiguration, and it left me with an enormous sense of peace and unity. After it, I worked and thought better and more clearly than I ever had before."

Others agreed that it was a religious experience of a supreme order *if* you were prepared for it, *if* you wanted the right things from it.

Well and good, I thought. If a drug under proper circumstances did expand the spirit as well as the mind, did remove the hostilities so destructive to all of us, it would be as desirable as under the wrong conditions it could be dangerous. But what filled me with unease was the formlessness, the apparent lack of frame and reference, that seemed to characterize this community of experienced and intelligent users. How could internal purity coexist with external clutter, inward beauty tolerate outward ugliness? Was it enough to *be* without *doing*, to *feel* without *acting?* How could these ostensibly good people live in this hideous house even for two days without an immense urge to make it beautiful and clean with their own hands?

A mile away, on a hill outside the Castalia estate, I had seen a clapboard New England farmhouse, white and simple. Whatever their religious experience, those who built it did so out of their own sense of order and with full consciousness. Could this new breed evolve, through the taking of drugs, a new and equally valid tangible order? Until it did, perhaps faith should await evidence and the test of prolonged and rigorously controlled research.

Of this particular group at Castalia, only two could have been called esoteric or exotic. One was a blond-bearded man (later arraigned with his wife for possession of marijuana) who, we learned, was an Air Force major before he underwent a religious awakening and became a Hindu mystic. The other was a Tibetan monk.

The Tibetan monk came into the kitchen shortly after I had arrived, clad in long brown robes with a sort of loose coat over them. He was very tall with a shaven blond head and one blind eye — the result, I later learned, of an accident in India. Although he talked with an indefinable accent, he was an American who had left Harvard as a student, gone to India, and been converted to Buddhism by a Tibetan holy man. Now he lived at the Tibetan Lamasery in New Jersey. He seemed ill at ease that Saturday morning, very anxious to speak privately to Leary and then hitch a ride back to New York as soon as possible.

Leary later told us the cause of his anxiety. The young man had told him that he felt so full of negative reactions from the place that he had to leave. He told Leary that in the critical position Leary was now in, it "was wiser—even essential—for him to give up his fight against the authorities and withdraw from his position of leadership in the LDS movement. When two dogs fight over a bone," said the monk, "and one of them drops the bone, the other will drop it too and walk away."

Talking about this later, Leary said that he was inclined to concede the wisdom of this advice, but others said, "No, no, Tim, you can't do that! We can't do without you, you can't just go to prison."

Long before I heard of the monk's reactions, I was having my own negative charges. I took a long walk around the paths and hills of Castalia and wondered why. It was not the people, although in spite of their communal warmth there was a perceptible distance between them and an outsider like myself, due partly to a difference of generations and partly, I was sure, to the fact that they had experienced LSD and I had not.

One of the reasons for my feeling of anxiety, so strong that I too was on the verge of returning to New York that night, was, I suspected, a lifelong aversion to communal life as such, to the perpetual flux and talk, and to the sheer physical dreariness of the house. Before knowing where I was to sleep that night, I was shown at least twelve of the many bedrooms. Equipped with one recently occupied mattress, a chair, and little else, they filled me with middle-class dismay. The one I thought was destined for me had one wall painted over entirely with a huge slit-eyed Eastern idol, and the thought of sleeping or waking in its presence was not palatable. Fortunately, the library — large and booklined, with two actual beds — was made available, although the events of the night made even such comforts rather irrelevant.

The house might not be to my taste, and the way of living in it not mine, but what really disturbed me finally became clear. It was something about Leary himself.

What? Here was a man in firm control of body and intellect, a man of wit, of courage if also of foolhardiness, of a wide range of knowledge. His well-worn library bore some evidence of this in its variety and scope: books on religion with strong emphasis on the Eastern faiths, psychiatry, psychology, extrasensory perception, history, anthropology, zoology, magic, geology; the works of Tolstoy, Dostoevsky, Freud, Plato, Toynbee, Maurois, T. E. Lawrence, William Blake; books on semantics, mysticism, plant growing. (By a window were boxes full of seedlings — pansy, phlox, alyssum.)

Leary, accompanied by men and youths with power saws and axes, spent most of that Saturday clearing out the center of what he called the "sacred grove" of tall firs not far from the house on a hill. In between, he himself did much of the tidying of the house, while assigning others to special jobs. He was courteous and watchful and never without a closely listening audience.

That was perhaps one clue to my unease: the feeling of cult, of master and disciple. It was intensified when he and his son Jack held a long dialogue, also in public; an exchange not only cryptic to the uninitiated but full of a kind of jargon I was beginning to recognize as common to the LSD group. What was essentially private dialogue, since it was obviously a father-son sparring, had become a public exhibition, somehow spurious.

Then too, that Saturday in the kitchen Leary played the tape recording of his interview the night before on the Barry Gray show on WMCA. He had been pitted against Dr. Donald B. Louria, chairman of the narcotics subcommittee of the New York County

Medical Society, and others in a long and sometimes acrid discussion on the implications of LSD and the problems of controlling its use. It was not so much the fact of playing the tape (for most wanted to hear it) but the content of Leary's arguments that somehow seemed facile in view of the charges made. To the others, however, each of his statements drew audible approval, while those of the opposition, measured as some were, brought impatient or contemptuous response.

It was an important argument: where can the line between individual right and public safety be drawn? Leary claimed that every human being has the right to extend his own consciousness, to gain insight into himself, to experience change, to reach religious revelation, provided he does this within the confines of his own home. His opponents conceded the right to private experience but doubted strongly that it was possible to guarantee that the individual undergoing LSD would *not* go outside his home, with possible harm to others. As to self-harm — and all, including Leary, agreed that taking the drug without proper preparation and supervision could be harmful — opinions varied sharply as to the incidence of such harm in relation to the numbers of its users. (A psychiatrist there told us that one injection of a certain substance could immediately alleviate violently adverse reactions in a subject; hence the required presence of a trained "sitter" or supervisor.)

Leary himself insists that LSD should not be taken by those not previously prepared and trained for it, and without this supervision. But he maintained throughout the program that the potentially beneficial effects of contemplation, examination, and revelation far outweigh the potential dangers.

"They don't understand," said the young father feeding his infant from a bottle while he listened to Leary's opposition on the tape. "They just don't know what they're talking about."

Yet, as I watched Leary listening to himself, my negative reactions persisted. Something was lacking, some essential element of leadership. Lacking to me, perhaps, but apparently not to those who had taken LSD, who sat at his feet, who gave him their unstinted loyalty.

Leary was certainly not sinister. He seemed an open — yes, a naïve — man, and perhaps his tragedy was that the very nature of the drug he had brought into such prominence had such strong appeal to those less responsible than he: not the group at Castalia but the young beats in the schools and cities, the unstable, the lost.

If there was nothing sinister about Leary, neither was there about the group at Castalia that weekend, or their activities on the night of the raid.

My roommate, a distinguished woman who, like me, was an outsider, never having taken LSD or been to Castalia before, told me of what they did after I had gone to bed:

"We all went up to the fir grove and sat in a circle around the bonfire made from the wood the men had cut down all day, and we sat there, just feeling very peaceful and happy. Sometimes we sang, sometimes we talked, or were quiet and just looked at the fire and up at the stars."

Then she too, some time after eleven, went to bed, and I heard from the others what they did in Leary's room — the one above ours — until the police broke in.

"We sat around in Tim's room," one man said, "and looked at some films M— —had made. They were in color and they were about several things. One was about parachute jumping, one was about water insects, and the other... oh yes, it was showing kids jumping on the trampoline here. They were really beautiful — he used all sorts of slowdown and speedup effects and angle shots, you know; he took the kids from below, sideways, the sort of thing..."

Then he laughed: "It was so sort of peaceful and pleasant I fell asleep. So did a couple of others. Right there, on the floor."

"But what about the music I heard from below?" I asked. "It had a strong beat. I thought you were dancing there."

"God, no," he said, "that was the sound track." Others told me this too, and one said, "Some orgy!"

After the police came, all the group agreed that the troopers and sheriffs expected an orgy and found it hard to convince themselves that this time, at least, none had existed. They looked at the messy house, they looked at the mattresses and the clutter and the guttering candles and the human assortment with expressions that mirrored the aversion they must have felt as they compared it with their own tidy homes and the ordered life they knew. The mattresses alone were symbols of sin and depravity. It had probably not occurred to them that, quite apart from the shared belief, expressed at Castalia, that lying on the floor is natural and relaxing, conducive to peace, beds cost money and Leary didn't have any. Or that one of the reasons clothes were strewn on the floor was the absence of furniture to put them on or closet space to hang them in. The [to me] regrettable lack of an aesthetic sense in "free" people and the young was only partly responsible. "Things are not important," said an eighteen-year-old.

"I had gone to sleep," said one man, "when the troopers wrenched open the door, shouted at me to get up, and started going through everything I had. I was half-asleep, but I knew they thought I was drugged and treated me like it."

Next morning over coffee and bacon, there was repeated talk about "Well, here we go — the midnight knock on the door...like in Germany" or "What kind of a world do we live in anyway?" Or "the poor damn cops didn't have a clue."

The psychiatrist agreed, but maintained that on the whole the police had behaved very correctly. True, they expected to find much more than they got; true, they disliked intensely what they saw; but certainly, after all the well publicized Leary troubles and LSD focus, the raid was inevitable.

Part II

As a
Commentator

Part II

As a
Commentator

An Egomaniac
Artist's Prayer
(1926)

O Lord, may I be bigoted until the end of my days,
that I may see and follow only one way, and not twenty.

O Lord, may I be arrogant as to smother the abject
humility within me.

O Lord, may I be ruthless, to trample over the men and
women who impede my forward-going.

O Lord, may I be callous, that the sad faces of the men
and women trampled under by me may not rise in the
night and tear my heart.

O Lord, may I be blind, so as not to perceive this bigotry
and arrogance, ruthlessness and utter callousness, but
that I may believe, finally, in my own invincible divinity.

VALEDICTORY
(AT THE VELTIN SCHOOL, MAY 25, 1923)

...You are young, and youth is vigor, and vigor means continual growth, continual progress. Sweep the world before you as a great wind sweeps the land. Go. Gain wisdom from experience, foresight through enthusiasm, and reserve power through unbounded love, for only through giving will you receive.

And when you look back at the radiance of your youth, do not weaken with vain regrets.

UTOPIA

(A short play written for
Mannes's commence-
ment at the Veltin School,
performed by actors from
her class on
May 23, 1923.)

Time: Age of Pericles

Place: Academy at Athens, Greece

Characters: Plato
        Six Pupils:
                Aristotle
                Isocrates
                Themistocles
                Hippocrates
                Stupidites
                Nuttocles

Enter Plato, fuming, attired in sheet and fillet, and followed by his entire class, similarly garbed.

PLATO *[pacing wildly]:* By Zeus and Ox-eyed Hera, I will not stand for it. To think that most of you are sixteen years old, and have mastered only logic, rhetoric, mathematics, and music, when you should have disposed of those trifling subjects at the age of ten. I must take drastic steps to mitigate this unspeakable condition. *[Stands still]* Come here, Stupidites. I have always thought you were the stumbling block of this class, and now I shall prove it. Stupidites, what are you?

STUPIDITES: I am human.

PLATO: What do you mean by human?

STUPIDITES: One who lives, and consists of eyes, ears, a nose, a mouth, and a stomach.

PLATO: O white-armed Pallas, what a definition! Begone, Stupidites. I'll have no more defectives to check our progress here. You possess an unpardonable sin: you never ask a question. When I asked you what you were, you should have replied, "What do you mean by 'what'?" Begone. *[Exit STUPIDITES]* Now that the hindering element has departed, we may resume our discussions on life. Aristotle, what have you observed lately of life and of those who enjoy it?

ARISTOTLE: I have observed, master, that those who educate the young question *them* but never question themselves.

PLATO: An excellent, if irreverent, observation. Why do you think this is so?

ARISTOTLE: Because, usually only those instruct who think they have found the answers to nearly everything, and having found them, consider their searching over, and become as static as the stars in the sky.

PLATO: You possess a glimmering of the truth. Little Nuttocles, what have you been thinking of?

NUTTOCLES: I have been thinking how very pleasant it is not to think.

PLATO: Ha! Define "pleasant."

NUTTOCLES: By pleasant, I mean soothing to the senses, and to the brain.

PLATO: Define "brain."

NUTTOCLES *[verging on tears]:* Oh, master, I do not know what "brain" is, other than a necessary evil.

PLATO: Pull yourself together, retire to the inner court, and commit the first book of the *Iliad* to your memory. That will be as soothing to your senses as vacancy, and far more constructive. Isocrates, you look dissipated. What have you been doing all day and all night?

ISOCRATES: And why should you know, master?

PLATO: Because, in order to remove the effect, one must eradicate the cause.

ISOCRATES: Why remove the effect?

PLATO: Because dissipation is not beautiful to look upon, and therefore sinful. Come now, explain.

ISOCRATES: I had lunch with Amnesia, went to the Aristophanes comedy with Castoria, supped with Aspasia, banqueted with Alcibiades, made love to Anemia, and then—

PLATO: Enough. I shall send you to Sparta to become a soldier, if you show a milky face in this academy again.

THEMISTOCLES: Master, we are pale because you give us too much to do. There is a limit to all things, as you remarked yesterday while discoursing on eating.

PLATO: I stand corrected, if what you say is true. You should not be made pale and unlovely with work in your youth. To continue our discussion, what have you been thinking of, Hippocrates?

HIPPOCRATES: Master, this woman Sappho is an outrage, part of this dangerous feminist movement now springing up.

HIPPOCRATES [*as if Plato were deranged*]: Woman was created merely to further the race of man.

PLATO: Out, you ignorant cub. The only charge against the female sex is that one of them bore you.

THEMISTOCLES: Master, anger is not beautiful to look upon, and therefore, sinful.

PLATO: You may follow your classmate, Themistocles. I allow no impudent remarks here. Before you leave, arrange your draperies. You look like an unmade bed.

[Exit THEMISTOCLES, making a long nose at PLATO]

PLATO: *[after a head count]:* By this interesting process of elimination, we may finally attain a state of peaceful and sincere learning. The more people, the less the average intelligence. Therefore, my dear pupils, you may all be dismissed.

[All exeunt] What use is this glory of mind, if there is none to realize it, to absorb it, to applaud it. *[calling after pupils]* Come back, at once. Plato has need of you.

[The class troops in] I've been a little too harsh on you. In my desire to inculcate wisdom, I have neglected to encourage folly, which is one of the most precious things in life. Let's sing praises to Bacchus and his merry throng. Come now, make it lively.

[party time]

Curtain

LETTERS HOME
FROM LONDON
(1923)

The first morning of my nineteenth year was spent in the studio of Dobson, sculptor, in the arduous task of cutting down a block of stone to a required size with the aid of two chisels and two hefty mallets, used alternately. I enjoyed myself hugely doing this purely menial work, even though my wrist is still weak from the effort. Believe me, sculpture is great exercise. I stood and hacked away for two and a half hours. I was absolutely famished when I reached Hampstead after an hour's bus ride, and stowed away an incredible amount. Dobson is terribly nice. He has a sense of humor and sympathy, and leaves one alone. He interrupted me during the morning only once or twice to show me how to put a patina on bronze fresh from the foundry. He heated up the little bronze figure with a gas flame until it steamed, then painted it with a greenish copper solution. The resulting finish was a beautiful rich, brown-gold, very satisfying and gorgeous.

Dobson wants to make me familiar with the carving tools. He says I'm doing the same things on that hunk of stone that one does in any stone sculpture. Monotony differentiates the two.

I forgot to tell about my lunch at the 1917 Club. All of the women had stringy short hair and wore sloppy clothes and smoked incessantly. Most of the men were very attractive, with thick thatches of hair and strong Celtic faces. They all knew each other. My friends and I are all of the monarchist party and consequently felt rather out of place in that den of labour and anarchy. I admire them for their sincerity, but I'm positive they're on the wrong track.

When I returned home Friday, I was so dog-tired in my arms and legs that I flopped on the sofa and slept for an hour and a half. In the evening the Reeces, Kitty, and I went to the Blue Bird, which is a Russian company parallel to the Chauve-Souris. The Kallins know all the actors and consequently got us free seats. The director does the sort of thing Balieff does. At first I thought he was merely a rank imitation, but I came to the conclusion that he was finer. He talks pidgin English, but much more subtly.

Last night was spent in front of the fire talking, and hearing John read his Van Gogh. We all retired early to stock up for the rest of the week. tonight I dine with Mr. Maule and the Osbournes at a very swell little restaurant called The Ivy, a place frequented by Barrie and other high lights.

I am amazed at the freedom of speech in English newspapers. They stop at nothing in slandering statesmen right and left. It is really wonderful, the liberty over here. I do think it's the freest country in the world. One could walk down Bond Street in evening slippers and a monocle, no more, and yet not be given a look.

Incidentally, the Tories chucked Lord Birkenhead, much to the delight of everyone. He is considered the archfiend of England. The papers said that the Conservatives wished to get rid of second-class brains, and therefore gave Birky the boot.

Your birthday letters were great. I should write to each member of the family in reply to their letters, but I'm too lazy, and I suppose, or hope, you don't object to this wholesale correspondence of mine.

If it isn't extravagant or complicated, please send over Grace's book, after you've read it. Of course, if it's rotten stuff, don't bother. Sorry about domestic problem at home.

This morning I gave a fencing lesson to Kitty, who is dying to learn. It's rather fun teaching, and I'll benefit by it in more than one way. After that arduous work, I designed an Ariel fancy-dress costume for Kitty, and made a required sketch of my plasticine model. The weather is so horribly damp and chilly that there's no pleasure in going out, so I hug the gas stove and do odd jobs.

I'm furious because Clive Bell came to see John yesterday afternoon while I was at the market. Perhaps you know that nearly everybody here loathes Bell. Dorothy, who is too healthy-minded to live, can't breathe the same air with him. It seems that Henry James calls him a "parcel of filth" and he evidently fits the title. He, his former wife, Duncan Grant, Maynard Keynes, the economist, and Lupokova the ballet dancer change off living with one another, and no one knows whose child is which or vice-versa. Some ménage.

Saturday evening, we all played poker till late. Don't you know by this time that red cheeks are not for me? Red nose, yes, but let it go at that. I manage to keep warm even though the transition from bed to clothes is rather ghastly.

About Rome. I am beginning to be known here. So kindly banish all thought of the Eternal City just yet. I'm dying to go, but not this winter. *Comprends-tu?*

By the way, I wish you wouldn't tell me not to worry about my work or anything, and to drop it off—if I want. This makes it very hard for both of us, since I must make my living eventually, and want to. Treat me as you would a boy. I bet you never told Leopold not to worry about his music. You see, the less that's expected of you, the less you do. Expect me to write "the American Play" or evolve a new sculptural technique, and I may do so. And I've seen enough homes to realize that marriage need not stop important work on the female side. Even that is so far off, why consider it! At present nothing worries me but my ignorance. I live, work, and enjoy myself, and take what comes. Here endeth lesson number one.

I wrote Jo a long letter and don't see why he didn't get it. I have not yet acquired an English Jo and don't expect to. Though Jo is by no means the millennium, I have found no youth, however nice, with half his brains and sensibilities. I won't say I shan't, but them's my opinions.

I went to Parliament yesterday. The debate, unintelligible to me, was about amendments to a Trade Insurance Act and pertained to the current docker's strike. Tom Shaw, Minister of Labour, spoke bluntly and forcefully, a fuzzy-haired little Welshman (Labour) spoke passionately. Liberal and Conservative members spoke for the most part suavely and insinuatingly, while Labourites spoke like the bourgeois they evidently were. Among the more important debators were: Commander Kenworthy, Liberal for Hull, a huge, black-haired, sleek man with a soft voice and biting, vindictive sarcasm; Dr. MacNamara, Liberal for Camberwell, a horrible, heavy-lidded vulture of a man of whom Balfour is said to have remarked, "If he had more brains, he would be a half-wit"; Margaret Bondfield, Undersecretary of Labour, a fine-faced woman with a beautiful low voice, who spoke briefly and impersonally and certainly was a credit to her sex. When she rose to talk, she was greeted by "hear, hear" from all over the House, which continued throughout her short speech. Sidney Webb sat next to the Prime Minister, but neither of them spoke while we were there. What struck me most about the whole thing were: the untidiness of the hall and the slovenliness of most of the members, who slouched on the benches with their hands clasped around their stomachs as if to keep them from dropping their legs; the way Baldwin put his feet on the desk; the comparative erectness and attentiveness of the Labour members; the way several Tories kept their top hats on; the petty animosities given voice in every speech except that of the woman's; the crying of "order, order" to drown out a disapproved speaker; the way the members slouched in and out incessantly, bowing each time to the Speaker; Asquith sticking his head through the door and retreating quickly; the luxuriant hair growth of Labour Members as opposed to the baldness of the others (due, I suppose, to the formers' inability to pay for top hats and their more active life).

And to think that these funny little runts run the British Empire.

Lloyd and Ethel came to dinner, and we all went to the Everyman Theatre, about three minutes from Lawn House, to see *The Mask and the Face,* an adaptation from the Italian farce of Luigi Chiarelli by an American named Fernald. It was entertaining, though very artificial, and in spots, excessively coarse. The acting was excellent throughout. I took D. and Kitty, just to indulge myself. I must play the millionaire sometimes.

Awfully mad to have missed *Majestic*. Thought it sailed tomorrow.

REVIEW OF
RUTH DRAPER
(1929)

We need no spiritualistic séances to give us the miracle of materialization. Ruth Draper alone on a stage is enough for that. Given a chair, or a bench, or a shawl, she can create out of nothingness a questioning judge, a streetwalker, an altar, two girls bicycling, a horde of children. Her own impersonations, however brilliant, are perhaps the lesser part of her genius. There might be others who could change from banal society woman to toothless hag, from flouncing flapper to rasping horsewoman. But there is no one, we'll wager, who can make a crowd of people see human beings who exist only in the intensity of Ruth Draper's imagination. There is something uncanny and terrible about it.

When the curtain of the Comedy Theater first went up on two chairs against a semicircle of curtains, your correspondent sighed to herself, *"That* is stage design." And when Miss Draper came out and began to talk, she added, *"That* is theater." O lavish, idiotic, myopic producers, see that and scrap your million props. Understand, too, that no amount of lights and wigs and revolving platforms can snap a cheap play into life or a stupid actor into significance.

All of Miss Draper's sketches gave hilarious delight. The horsy woman in "An English Houseparty" and the Boston tourist and English lady-watercolorist of a sketch called "In a Church in Italy" are the stuff and essence of acute comedy. Real comedy is an art ten times more subtle and difficult than tragedy, and to make people laugh with joy is no easy matter. Miss Draper can move to tears, sometimes because she understands the human comedy so well, and because she comprehends human sentimentality even better. A sketch of a high-voiced little English girl I thought real tragedy. But in the "Thames Embankment" one, for instance, I found myself resenting the moisture in my eyes; it was too much like the tears some plaintive movies extort from me. If there is any criticism of Miss Draper as an artist, it might be that her shawl has grown to be a too-invariable symbol of this pathos. Perhaps if it were used less often, or if another symbol, as simple and telling, were found...But that is hyper-criticism, verging on the eclectic. Miss Draper is too rare an experience for carping.

HYDE PARK

Ten years have passed and still the hate is green
As the grass around the grave; and still the dogs
Scrabble in whining frenzy in the mud
For the fresher bones of blame. This is a time
When nobody speaks of you except in ire and those who loved
Keep silent. This is a time
Of no memorials and a foreign shrine
Defaced. Your name's
No use to anyone now and is not used
But cursed. But quiet now, and still;
Quiet and still as thousands who walk by
And look with love and homage where you lie.

THE QUEEN'S AUNT
BY MARRIAGE

Review of The Heart Has Its Reasons: The Memoirs of the Duchess of Windsor (McKay; Hardbound price in 1956, $5)

To say that Wallis Windsor's book is a good deal better than one expected may be faint praise, but it is praise nevertheless. For the expectation was that her story of her life would be shallow, vain, trivial, and defensive, and it is none of these. The severest criticism that can be leveled at the writing itself is that it is colorless, sometimes boring, and generally overgroomed, not a reaction out of place or a fumble showing. It is at once a candid and careful book, for though the Duchess is quite honest about the compelling fascination grand society held for her, the unswerving ambition that led her to seek it throughout her life is not admitted. The tragic union that crowned it appears rather as the result of a sequence of fateful happenings.

The book makes only too clear the common fault of this couple: lack of judgment. Whether it concerns the friends they choose or the acts they perform (their appalling trip among the Nazis in Germany in 1937 is a prime example), their personal and political naïveté is astonishing in two people so much of the world. In the case of the Duchess especially, only a deep ignorance of British history and character could have made her so shocked and surprised at the royal family's total rejection of her and the abdicated king she married, a rejection that no preceding decency of motive on her part and no ensuing devotion to her husband could ever erase.

The irony is that the devotion so palpable in this book cannot disguise her royal husband's fatal flaw: that willful and mutinous obstinacy which in the end neutralized his many fine qualities, so that now they are neither useful nor used.

What remains to these two, and this is what makes the story so tragic, is things: houses, furniture, clothes, and food. In all of these they show the taste so absent in their choice of people.

The Duchess often mentions the inherent sadness in the Duke's face, an expression apparent even at his life's crest. He lived in a closed and lonely world which only she, it appears, could open, warm, and inhabit. It would seem that only his flowers and his dogs inhabit that world today.

THE RIGHT
TO BE
ENTERTAINED

There was once a king called Addlehead I. According to legend, he called his jester to him one day and said, "See to it that I am entertained from morning to night every day of the week, including Sunday. I wish perpetually available for my pleasure, singers, dancers, funny men, mimes, acrobats, and accomplished children and dogs. It does not matter what they perform so long as I am diverted."

So the jester complied with his monarch's wish. King Addlehead, diverted all day and night, including Sundays, ceased to govern and his people fell into misery and named him Addlehead the Imbecile.

History, however, can reverse itself. Many years later there was a great and powerful country where each citizen was a king like Addlehead, able to be diverted all day and all night, including Sundays. Only those who were so entertained were not called imbeciles; they were merely television viewers.

There is no legend in the fact that for the first time in any era in any country on earth, a whole people has found it not only desirable but natural to be constantly entertained. No one has questioned whether it *is* natural or desirable. Only the nature of the entertainment, whether good or bad, has been examined. Not one voice has asked, "Why should we be constantly entertained?

I know in my own youth that we went to a play only four or five times a year, and to a movie never more than once a fortnight. These were excitements long anticipated and remembered. The thought of having them constantly accessible never entered the mind. Nowadays it seems preposterous *not* to avail oneself constantly of diversion,

115

since a flick of a knob can produce it.

I do not propose to draw any somber conclusions from this fact of our civilization, except to point out that the whole man or woman does not need or want this constant diversion. That is why, except for professionals concerned either productively or critically with the media, you will find very few people of spiritual or mental substance who turn on television or radio more than a few hours a week. For them, to turn on a quiz show or soap opera during the day would be unthinkable, an act of self-imposed boredom. One glimpse of this suffocating surfeit of entertainment (and who in illness has not had it?) is enough to cure any random viewer.

The producers of television will never ask themselves whether it is right that people should be entertained four-fifths of the day and informed one-fifth, or whether the reverse might be palatable. They never will ask themselves this so long as the majority of commercial programs depend on selling goods. For you can't sell if you don't entertain, and a two hundred million Addleheads are two hundred million consumers.

We ourselves might ask: Why do we need to be diverted? And from what? Are we not the happiest people in the world?

TV LESSON

The experts instructed the politi-
cians . . . in the techniques of dressing,
talking, gesturing, and looking sincere . . .

Look the camera in the eye,
Keep the chin-line firm,
Sit with nonchalance and try
Not to shift or squirm.

When you speak of origins,
Family, or life,
Cultivate the boyish grin
That won your girlish wife.

Let the mouth be grim and straight
When you talk of prayer,
Morality, the Soviet State,
And Freedom Everywhere.

Never rise above your kind
Even if you could:
To have an ordinary mind
Is for the common good.

All this you should know by now,
The model has been clear:
It's never what you say, but how
You make it sound sincere.

HELEN KELLER

It took an old medium, an old woman, and old truths to wash away, at least for an hour, the dirt that has settled on us during the last months. In *The Unconquered,* the story of Helen Keller, a blind woman shows us how to see, a deaf woman shows us how to listen, a great woman shows us how to be humble. This short film, done with the utmost restraint and sensibility, is in a way a religious experience in that we are permitted to share that ecstasy of goodness which is one definition of sainthood.

We may know that Helen Keller has been deaf, blind, and mute since an illness in the nineteenth month of her life, that she has devoted her life to the similarly afflicted, that she is a famous American. Many of us have left it at that, turning away from the thought of her with that mingled pain and guilt that the afflicted arouse in us. It hurts us that we can do nothing for them; we are guilty because we are whole. I suppose that a great many people will avoid this picture for those reasons. But they will make a profound mistake.

For this documentary breathes affirmation; there is in it not one ugly or negative thing. Helen Keller's face itself has an extraordinary beauty, from the sightless delicacy of her girlhood to the transfiguration of her seventies. It is the face of love. And the miraculous thing about this woman is that she transfigures those with whom she comes in contact, whether it is her lifelong companions or afflicted strangers. In repose, the sockets of the blind and the contorted mouths of the dumb can be painful to watch. In the presence of Helen Keller, joy and communication give them an inner light that extinguishes the pain.

The narration, spoken beautifully, free from mannerisms or emphasis, by Katharine Cornell, takes us through Miss Keller's entire life: a triumphant progress of the human spirit from total isolation to total community. I doubt whether even the most compassionate and imaginative can project themselves into the state she lived as a little girl: a world of wholly soundless darkness out of which consciousness could not even voice its despair. That she escaped from it was due not only to her courage and intelligence, but to a young Boston girl named Annie Sullivan, who led her out of her prison by teaching her first how to communicate with her hands, and then with her voice.

For fifty years, these two lived hand in hand, finger to finger, dedicated not only to each other but the spiritual expansion of the physically limited. And when Annie Sullivan died, another remarkable woman, Polly Thompson, took her place as Helen Keller's other self.

To see them together during the hours of their day on their Connecticut hill is both moving and liberating, touching not in the sense of pathos, for there is nothing remotely pathetic about Helen Keller, but in the sense of sweetness, warmth, and gaiety. Fingers racing in palm, they read their mail together, have their jokes, plan their days, speak to their friends.

There is almost always a smile on Helen Keller's face, whether (with hand on set) she "listens" to radio, whether she dries the dishes Polly has washed, or types her letters (she uses both Braille and standard), or goes on her daily walk, guided by the thousand feet of wooden handrail her friends have built for her. On this walk she is alive to everything: the sun on her face, the twig in her path, the bud on the bush, the herbs at her feet. She touches everything, everything touches her. No seeing, hearing being could know more of creation or love it more.

Each day begins with her fingers reading the Braille Bible; each day ends with it spread open under her moving hands in the room where she sleeps. her face then has infinite joy.

In between these periods of seclusion, Helen and Polly travel to the ends of the earth on their mission of help. No one alive, perhaps, has met more of the world's endowed and more of the world's afflicted. And wherever she goes, this blind, deaf woman, light floods the darkness, pride and hate dissolve, kindness prevails. Helen Keller can make it seem that humanity is indeed created in the image of God.

A DISSONANT
DIALOGUE

They were sitting around, eight of them, listening to records of contemporary music. One was a composer, one a pianist, two a man and wife dedicated to the support of modern American music, one a teacher of composition, two students, and a woman with a troubled look. When the last record had ended and there was a pause punctuated by low murmurs of appreciation, she said, "Do you think we could play a little Mozart now?"

They turned to look at her, jarred.

"Still unconvinced?" said the pianist.

"Don't worry about her," said the patron-host. "She just likes to graze in old pastures."

"I don't know if I care for that image," said the woman, "but frankly, I don't think I can take any more of what we've been hearing."

"What do you think we've been hearing?" asked the teacher.

"Wanderings," said the woman, "interminable wanderings in sound, interrupted now and then by excursions into noise."

"How about a drink, everybody?" said the hostess, rising. "What'll you have?"

The rest gave their orders and split into intense little analytical groups. The woman was left alone, exiled, she felt, with her trouble, until the composer came over and sat next to her. As they talked, she remarked that modern music did not make her think of anything except the composer's poverty of soul and the end of his piece, should that ever arrive. She said that if she suspected talent running through his incoherence, she was angry because of the effort involved in discovering it. If there was no talent, merely a pretentious use of the most rigid modern idiom, she was even angrier.

"In other words, you find it disturbing because you don't understand it."

"If so," she said, "I am in a majority, a much greater majority than those who still flinch at Picassos and Legers. *Your* audience consists of a dedicated band of modern-music practitioners and lovers, augmented by a slightly larger group of people who find it fashionable to pretend that they understand it."

"In the absence of a Gallup Poll on the subject," said the composer, with an edge to his voice, "I can only say that this majority of yours must be more obtuse than I thought."

The woman, calm until now, exploded. "There we go again. The assumption by avant-garde painters and composers that people must learn *their* language, never that *they* must first learn to speak to people! This is the supreme arrogance: 'Here's my cipher, boys, come and decode it.' I used to believe that art was a form of communication."

The composer tried to be patient. "Do you expect a young talent writing today to copy Schubert and Chopin? What can he do but reflect the world he lives in?"

"Reflect?" she said. "Not exactly. I expect any artist to do two things: accept the past and fuse the present. In an age of incessant change, he needs classic reaffirmation of constant values. Most of all, I expect him to know his head and his ears, and the connection between them. If a man doesn't know what he wants to say, or has nothing to say, no chorus of typewriters, dinner gongs, steam drills, squash gourds, or oscillating chants that moan on for hours is going to help him. Neither is a beat outside the range of human experience."

"I don't know what you're talking about," said the composer. "What would you call a beat *inside* the range of human experience?"

The woman thought for a moment. "Well, the beat of the heart, the rhythm of breathing. There they are, in everyone; definite, regular, inevitable. This beat, this breathing, must have its echo in music."

"Dum-de-de-dum, dum-de-de-dum," said the composer, scornfully.

"Don't be silly. Why are great melodies never forgotten? They are literally and figuratively, man's aspiration. It's the same with great poetry; it has the cadence of the heart. But take so much of contemporary music. It is a pant, a stutter, a stammer. You people seem to have some disease of the soul. Your progression in music is one of fits and starts; it stumbles and wavers, gibbering as it goes. And even when it has a clear direction, it is so often one of assault, a series of jabs and punches designed to shock the ear into attention."

"You must come and hear my latest composition," said the composer, now at the limits of his tact.

"I always do," the woman said. "And afterwards, I will want to listen to *Don Giovanni*."

THEATER:
SOMETHING
UNSPEAKABLE

Scene: A garden, composed entirely of giant pitcher plants. A door, left, leads into an old Southern house. The air is filled with the strangled buzz of flies being trapped by the plants.

Characters: The PLAYWRIGHT, who looks like Tennessee Williams.

The DOCTOR, who looks like me

[When the curtain rises, the PLAYWRIGHT is under the influence of sodium pentothal. I am under the influence of the PLAYWRIGHT.]

ME: Give me your resistance. I want to have all your resistance.

PLAYWRIGHT *[drowsily, with his eyes half-closed]:* I am giving it to you.

ME: I want all the truth. I want you to tell me why you wrote *Suddenly Last Summer.*

PLAYWRIGHT: Because life is terrible and sweet and beautiful.

ME: What is beautiful?

PLAYWRIGHT: Words are beautiful. There is nothing more beautiful than words.

ME: What is terrible?

PLAYWRIGHT: Mothers are terrible. Relatives are terrible. Love is terrible.

ME: What is sweet?

PLAYRIGHT: The iridescence of decay is sweet. The odor of putrescence is sweet. The silence of audiences is sweet.

ME: What do you think about women?

PLAYWRIGHT: Women are either bitches or victims of bitches. If they have any goodness, it is destroyed.

ME: Go on.

PLAYWRIGHT: Their goodness destroys men as much as their evil does. Women betray themselves over and over in talk. I can hear them all of the time.

ME: What do you think about men?

PLAYWRIGHT: Men? Men are either ghosts or monsters. Virtue makes them ghosts; vice makes them monsters. Men cannot live without women and they have no future with women.

ME: Who has a future?

PLAYWRIGHT: Plants. Playwrights without hope.

ME: Tell me, did you really have to have your Sebastian eaten alive by starved children? Why?

PLAYWRIGHT: I like to appall.

ME: Why do you like to appall?

PLAYWRIGHT: People like to be appalled. It glues them to their seats.

ME: Can't you glue them to their seats without horror?

PLAYWRIGHT: It's harder. In a world of violence, people can be stirred only by violence. A torn mind is more shocking than a whole one. A torn body is more exciting than a whole one.

ME: What did you mean to say about *Suddenly Last Summer?*

PLAYWRIGHT: Say? I do not use the theater to say. I use the theater to enthrall. Magic need not have meaning. Who needs the reason for enchantment?

ME: I want to ask you about that other play about the two Southern women: *Something Unspoken.*

PLAYWRIGHT: Yes. What do you want to know?

ME: Why did you write that?

PLAYWRIGHT: It's good for actresses. They like to play bitches or the victims of bitches.

ME: Yes, but there must be something more to it than that.

PLAYWRIGHT: There is, something unspoken.

ME: Hate?

PLAYWRIGHT: You can label it that if you want.

ME: But isn't that rather a familiar relationship: the rich dominant woman and the timid crushed companion?

PLAYWRIGHT: Nothing is familiar with new words. Or no words.

ME: I'd like to ask you something else about that play.

PLAYWRIGHT: Yes?

ME: It's about Miss Alden, who plays the part of the companion. Her mouth is wide open most of the time, even when she isn't talking. Why?

PLAYWRIGHT: It's sort of a silent scream.

ME: Something unspoken?

PLAYWRIGHT: You might call it that.

ME: But she has it open as the mother in *Suddenly Last Summer*, too. And the girl in the play who "took her son away" is always talking, under sodium pentothal, of the black, open mouths of the starving Spanish children who eat Sebastian.

PLAYWRIGHT: Don't you find it a horrible image?

ME: I certainly do.

PLAYWRIGHT: Well?

ME: Tell me something: The dreadful mother in *Suddenly* wants the girl to have a lobotomy to rid her of her frightful vision.

PLAYWRIGHT: Yes?

ME: Would you like to be rid of your frightful visions?

PLAYWRIGHT: *[leaping up and out from under drug]:* Me? Good God, No! Where would I be without them?

Curtain

HEAVENLY
SWITCHBOARD

'Dial-a-Prayer—For a Spiritual Lift in a Busy Day'
> —sign on a New York church

Dial-a-Prayer. The Exchange is White House One-
0-0-0-0. You'll get an answer back
Quick as a jiffy; a psalm from Hagerty
Or a Hail from Hall; or, if the line is clear,
A Pater Noster from *him*.
Miraculous!
To phone for piety! But in this day
When values (moral and spiritual) have returned
(Thank God), people pray now.
Pay later. It's the American way.

REVIEW OF
WEST SIDE STORY

If talent and timing are the two major ingredients of success in all forms of art, I suspect that in theater timing is the more important of the two. It is *when* a play is produced that counts, for if the audience is not ready for it talent will not save it. And this is what makes producers shudder before an opening: Is it too late or too soon? Is it right for now?

Nothing could be more violent, more disturbing, and in some ways uglier than the structure of *West Side Story:* a story of delinquents, of the battle for the streets between the Puerto Rican "Sharks" and the indigenous "Jets," of the ferocious tensions of slum life in a jungle society. The miracle is the creative use of this material toward the improbable end of beauty. This Jerome Robbins and Arthur Laurrents and Leonard Bernstein have done, achieving, with the inspired settings of Oliver Smith, a most powerful work of art.

Robbins, director and choreographer, was the presiding magician, for he has turned the ritual hatreds of desperate kids into patterns of astounding beauty. Their raw movements have been clarifed and translated into dance: their strut, their insolent languor, their jive looseness, their dope-tightness, their ferocity. It is hard to see how a gang war on a racial basis can be anything but repellent and frightening. *West Side Story* is both, and yet it is also a classical ballet of death.

What might have been as mawkish as it is contrived — the Capulet-Montague love between the Puerto Rican girl and the "Jet" boy — is, miraculously again, neither. Instead it achieves moments of genuine purity. Mr. Bernstein's versatility is such that his music can be tender and melodic as well as frenzied and contrapuntal, and the musical would be unbearable if the relentless tension of the score were not relieved from time to time by simple song.

West Side Story is a tough evening in any case. But this exercise in violence is not an exploitation of sensation, pegged on delinquency headlines. It says something. It says that these young people are cramped, stifled, crazed by the walls around them. It says that even this violence has code and ritual. And it says, finally, that racial hatreds are nothing but the outward expression of terrible inadequacies within the haters.

The only thing Brendan Behan and Jean Anouilh have in common, aside from current productions on Broadway, is my apparent inability to pronounce their names. BeHAN (BEEhan?) tries hard not to write a play and succeeds. Anouilh (Ahnooey? Ennui?) tires hard to write a play and fails. Since he expects nothing of me, Behan gives me no sense of guilt at all. On the contrary, I become as irresponsible a spectator as he is a playwright. But with Anouilh I am insecure and guilt-ridden. I try very hard to understand what he is saying, and if I don't, I feel it is my fault. I sit there convincing myself that important truths are waiting in the wings and that I should be happy in such witty, literate, imaginative company, but my legs keep twitching and I find myself wishing I were somewhere else, preferably in a bar.

I know this is reprehensible, especially when I recognize irony and perception in so many lines. But *Becket,* Anouilh's study of the strange relationship between the boorish Henry II of England and the close companion who transferred the ardor of his loyalty from king to God, I suffered from the same malaise. My mind urged involvement, but my emotions lay dormant. I would be happy to see Sir Laurence Olivier playing the Seventh Dwarf in *Snow White,* and he had much better lines in *Becket;* the scenery of Oliver Smith and the costumes by Motley were wonderful. But quite aside from the general quality of the disengagement and anemia which (to me at least) spells the weakness of Anouilh, I was deeply disturbed by the difference in kind and timbre between the performances of Anthony Quinn as Henry and Olivier as Becket. Quinn is a fine actor, but he is wholly American not only in accent and intonation, but in bearing, walk, and gesture. I could not for one moment believe his presence as a Norman monarch, however uncouth and simple, or his relationship with the Saxon Becket. It confirmed once more my belief in the necessity of homogeneous style in any theater production, not merely in accent or mannerism alone, but in a common heritage of techniques and attitudes.

That there is no such discrepancy in *The Hostage* is one of its pleasures. The people Behan has thrown together in his Dublin boardinghouse-brothel are a cockeyed assortment, but they are unified not only by a close-knit cast but by the Irishman's love of them, his irrepressible good humor, and his roaring irreverence. For these his plot is a thin excuse, and I found myself at first rather pursing my lips at such wholesale flouting of dramatic disciplines, and even more at its Irishness, a little of which goes a long way with me. But the acting was so good, the lines were so funny, and the songs so blithely inserted for so little point that I let reason abdicate and Behan take over. It is, as many have said, no more than a romp. but it is not a stupid romp. And if I am grateful to Behan for anything more than that, it is his outrageous impudence toward the unmockable, whether it is the Church, chastity, or a simpler continence. He will not lower his voice, and for that I salute him.

REVIEW OF O'NEILL'S
LONG DAY'S
JOURNEY
INTO NIGHT

When a play by a great American dramatist receives a fine production and the almost unanimous praise of distinguished critics, it is not only hard but hazardous to give a dissenting opinion. Yet at the risk of losing stature and no risk of diminishing O'Neill's, this reviewer feels compelled to record certain reactions to *Long Day's Journey into Night* and to try to explain why, in her view, the play does not achieve the universality of tragedy in spite of a standard of feeling and writing that makes most contemporary drama trivial to the point of vacuity.

The reasons are inherent both in the story and in the treatment of this very long and grueling play, and I think they hinge on the words used by the playwright's widow in describing its genesis: "He was bedeviled into writing it," she said. "... He had to get it out of his system, he had to forgive whatever it was that caused this tragedy between himself and his mother and father."

Probably the essence of my divergence from majority opinion is just this: They feel that O'Neill *did* "get it out of his system" and into a higher realm of existence, and I feel he did not. To me, the Tyrone family remained O'Neill's family throughout, torn piece by piece from his guts; and it was in this very specialness that the play's shortcomings as tragedy stood revealed.

The Tyrone-O'Neill family is not only painful to look at but hard to identify with. There are four personal tragedies consummated in the writer's own tragedy, that of the perpetually haunted Eugene O'Neill. For this reason I found that I and (judging by the constant coughing) a number of others were seldom deeply affected by the despair in each Tyrone. We watched them brought to life by a superb company of actors, well aware of their suffering and their inexorable doom, but it was not *our* suffering and *our* doom—as I believe it might well have seemed in a less subjective and obsessive treatment of people so overfreighted with catastrophe. Again, this is a minority opinion: the play appears to move many people continuously, and they seem not to share a certain embarrassment at too intimate exposures of individual pain, specific wounds from which the eye averts itself.

My second objection to the play concerns its length. Some of the most enthusiastic reviews conceded repetitiousness and need of pruning as minor flaws, but others acclaimed the length as essential. Yet I would say that the extra hour does the play a real disservice, and that the many long harangues on familiar subjects become boring to the occasional point of impatience, of actual exasperation at repeated suffering.

Within the first hour of *Long Day*, the whole substance of the *Journey into Night* is known. We know that the father Tyrone is a weak, blustering miser, guilty in part of his wife's degradation and his son's despair, although he bears diverse kinds of love for them. We know that Mrs. Tyrone is a dope addict, incapable of cure in spite of sanitarium periods, immune to reality. We know that James, the older brother, is a psychotic drunk, torn between love and hate for young Edmund. We know that Edmund—O'Neill himself—is overvulnerable, tubercular, and racked by his family's torture. We know, without the shading of a doubt, that his family is doomed, sealed forever in the vault of their own errors and illusions.

What we learn during the next three hours is quantitative rather than qualitative; more, not different. There is nothing wrong with a cumulative sense of inevitability: It is the root of Greek tragedy. But I cannot help thinking that there is something wrong in terms of theater when foreknowledge is as complete as this, particularly if it is knowledge of hopelessness. This must impart a static condition of emotion, incapable of change or solution; and I would think tragedy could contain the first without necessarily providing the second.

What we have instead is nearly four hours of very slight variations in content and only one variation in pace — the repeated shift in the Tyrone relationships from violent recrimination to desperate affection; the voices at one moment loud and harsh, at the next low and tender. Thus one is yanked back and forth between the faces of love and hate until the texture of one's attention is limp and shredded.

I feel also — and strongly — that one or two outside elements (not members of the Tyrone family) would have done great service in putting the family in perspective and showing the outside of the cage as well as its dreadful interior. The young Irish maid did this to a certain extent, and so admirably in her scene with the drugged Mrs. Tyrone that I found myself grateful for her intrusion. I would have welcomed others.

It is clear that O'Neill wanted us to share his hell without this form of release, this breath of free outer air. But the play is rough enough on an audience without complete imprisonment in the Tyrone cell.

I would be the last to say that *Long Day's Journey* is without great moments. There are a number of scenes of human revelation, of agonizing honesty, that only great talent could create. Both in high and low key, O'Neill's speech can attain a riveting urgency, a brooding, inexorable passion.

If I have any criticism of what is otherwise a superb production, I would charge Director José Quintero and the cast with overplaying the written words, which are so powerful that they need neither volume nor emphasis for their projection. Only the stormy flights and loud extravagances of the father Tyrone and the son Jamie were exempt from restraint: Fredrick March and Jason Robards, Jr., take the honors of the evening.

As the old ruin of an actor, eaten by guilt and driven to his destructive miserliness by the memories of childhood penury, March makes a magnificent and pathetic Tyrone, the man the father O'Neill must surely have been. Robards as the elder son only confirms what his performance as the salesman in *The Iceman Cometh* amply proved: that he is an actor of enormous range and intensity. I could not imagine the young Edmund in better hands than those of Bradford Dillman, whose scene of mutual recognition with his father was one of the most moving in the play. If I leave Florence Eldridge to the last, it is not because she did not give her whole talents as the wife escaping through dope into a kinder past, but that somehow she did not come as close to Mrs. Tyrone as the image of her conveyed — to me, at least — by reading the play.

At times there was a pettishness in her that I did not perceive in the written character, who seemed essentially sweeter and warmer. I felt also that her Mrs. Tyrone was never really °there." Although this was the core of her tragedy, that she removed herself from reality by her addiction, I think there should have been more moments of deeper communication, if only to indicate what she once was, and to allow some identification with her torture. I am probably a minority of one in finding her last scene more grotesque than tragic. Given the kind of pre-entrance that O'Neill masterfully provided — a half hour of the men alone waiting in dread for what they knew must be her fearful entry — she appears with her white hair streaming over her eyes trailing her old wedding gown behind her, a senile Ophelia. Her doom was explicit enough without this kind of stage business.

If, after you read this, your desire to see *Long Day's Journey into Night* is strengthened rather than weakened, then I am glad. I agree with those who feel that it is a rare theatrical experience. But I do take issue with the judgment that it is a great play or a great tragedy. It is a study of extreme personal anguish by an important playwright, brilliantly produced but in need of editing.

LETTER
TO A GIRL

My dear daughter whom I never had,

Perhaps it is just as well that you do not exist because you would have had a tough time with me as a mother. For on top of the normal difficulties of an always complex relationship, I would have subjected you to a kind of thinking and feeling which would have put you at odds with the society in which you lived. I might even have pulled you out of this society at a certain age so that you might better be able to build up a resistance to some of its infections. I most certainly would have made you unhappy and lonely at a time when American girls are the queens of the world. Shall I tell you why?

For one thing, I should not start from the cradle assuming that because you were a girl you had only one road in life and one function. For you are not one entity, but several, having masculine qualities as well as feminine, bearing within you the infinite combinations, sexual, intellectual, physical, of past generations. When you were old enough to read, I would see that your range was complete and not confined to the girlish slop imposed on female children by normal parents. If you preferred to read about girls (which I doubt; boys are more fun), that would be your business. But the choice would have to be there, and the encouragement to experiment in many areas not confined to your sex.

I would dress you attractively, of course; but I would be far more disturbed at an early clothes-consciousness in yourself than the lack of it. I find little girls who are perpetually preening themselves, swinging little bags, talking about clothes, nothing more than embryo bitches, the calculating, not the hearty kind.

I would give you all the information on sex that you asked for, at any time in your development. But I would show obvious disgust with the kind of talk of dating and boyfriends that starts, in most American families, at the age of eight and becomes obsessive by the age of twelve. This is meretricious sex, imposed by a constant barrage of television, radio, movies, and magazines aimed indiscriminately at the young as well as the old. I am deeply disturbed by schoolgirls from twelve to sixteen who wear heavy makeup, tint their hair, and engineer their breasts. Not only are they coarsened; they miss a time of utmost importance, the age of innocence. I know I would have trouble in this country keeping you from using makeup until you were fifteen. But I would try, hard. I would also tell you that the longer you stayed away from bras the better. No healthy young body needs support. There is no need to push the body into shapes favored by fashion, or to substitute and eventually weaken the pelvic and pectoral muscles which were meant to support you.

But I would hope fervently that before you starting using makeup you would have gone through a plain stage where you were neither attracted to or by boys; where you dreamed of life on your own single terms. I would want you to paint or learn an instrument or a language, or study ballet. I would most certainly want you to relish good food and learn how to cook it. I would want wiser and older women and men to take an interest in your growing mind.

More than anything else, I would want you to be alone quite a lot. I would even want you to be miserable. This is because I feel it is the only way you will learn your identity. For I cannot believe that girls who are "adjusted," boy-crazy, attractive, and dated from the age of twelve have time to learn it. They are following a pattern imposed on them since birth: a mating dance which has no core of experience in love and which has as its goal a child-marriage. I wonder if adults are produced by children producing children.

As for the idea of starting to "go steady" in your adolescence, I call it a presposterous limitation of growth, curiosity, adventure, and fun. Poor girl who dances with one boy all evening, every date. How dull. And the only reason it is the accepted pattern now is not tender and touching fidelity but fear of being left alone; the worst, apparently, that can befall a girl. Yet I would tell you that an evening spent alone is infinitely preferable to an evening stuck with a bore. This is the major disaster.

I would hope that you were chaste until you were eighteen. After that I would be much more concerned with your heart than with your chastity. There is a lot of hypocritical nonsense being said about the dire consequences to the female of premarital sexual relations. They are supposed to endanger all hope of future happiness. I can only tell you that it depends entirely on their nature. If you are intimate with a boy, or man, purely out of curiosity or for what *you* can get out of it, sex can be a soiling and spoiling experience. If you love, or really think you love the man, if you want to give *him* love, sex can be an enrichment. Between a girl who gives herself for these reasons and out of a real affection for men, and the girl who withholds herself for purposes of ultimate gain (a wedding ring, or "security"), I prefer the morality of the former.

It would be a marvelous thing, something of a miracle, if you found at eighteen the permanent answer to your dreams of love. From my own observation, the women who have achieved it most successfully are the women who have loved a number of men and learned the difficult but rewarding art of living with them. Give me the generous woman every time. Certainly the bane of men's existence is the ungenerous one.

All this is rankest heresy. But it seems to me the only honest approach in a day when fear of pregnancy is no longer a deterrent to sexual intimacy, and when the young are incited to sex by everything they see, read, and hear.

So you see, my daughter who never was, you could have a rough time if you lived today unless, unlike your mother, you kept these attitudes to yourself. But if you did, you would not be my daughter, would you?

MY
SOPHISTICATED
MAN

I can remember no time in my life when a sophisticated man was not the object of my interest, if not my search. Unlike some women, I have never had the patience of an educator nor the zeal of a reformer. I prefer the finished product; not a man incapable of growth, but one who has managed to acquire those perceptions, tastes and attitudes which constitute, to me, sophistication.

What was my yardstick? Well, in younger days, my preliminary judgments were largely visual. If I were standing by the rail of an ocean liner, for instance, and saw that a male was bearing down on me, I would retreat if he wore any of these things: a pale cloth cap, basket-weave sport shoes, a shirt unbuttoned at the neck and exposing, usually, a bristling sprout of hair. Now my list of repellents, academically speaking, is increased formidably. It includes plastic raincovers on hats (I have seen them even on Shriner fezzes), jackets pulled down by the straps of heavy cameras, and pale, loose suits. On the beaches of the North in summer and the South in winter, I would beat a hasty withdrawal from men in matching patterned shorts and jackets or silly hats. And in bucolic parties alfresco, the fellow barbecuing in an apron printed with "Cordon Bleu" or "I Wear the Pants" will have to look elsewhere (which he usually does) for a female companion. I mention these trivialities of attire because I am convinced that a sophisticated man wouldn't be seen dead in them. They are, one and all, emasculators, and if there is anything which a worldly man cossets, it is his male dignity.

I maintain that a man who has never been exposed to other societies cannot be sophisticated. I am speaking of a reasonable familiarity with foreign cities and peoples, art and customs. For

139

sophistication to me suggests, primarily, a refinement of the senses. The eye that has not appreciated Michelangelo's *David* in Florence or the cathedral of Chartres is not a sophisticated eye. The hand that has not felt the rough heat of an ancient wall in Siena or the sweating cold of a Salzburg stein of beer is an innocent hand. So are the fingers that have not traveled, in conscious and specific savoring, over the contours of many different women.

Would you recognize this kind of man across the room? He's easy in his clothes. His hands are well-groomed, but not manicured. He does not laugh loudly or often. He is looking directly at the woman he speaks to, but he is not missing others as they enter; a flick of the eye does it. For in all ways this man is not obvious. He would no more appear to examine a woman from the ankles up than he would move his lips while reading. His senses are trained and his reflexes quick. And how did they get that way? From experience, observation, and deduction. He is educated in life.

Now what about that fellow over there, the one telling a long story rather loudly to a girl who would prefer not to hear it. He is not, of course, aware of this, since he is not only a little tight but unaccustomed to watching the reactions of women. He will look down the front of her dress but not see the glaze on her eyes. He has not been educated in observation. He is, according to the dictionary, unsophisticated in that he is natural and simple, lacking in experience. And this, again according to the dictionary, is a compliment. For the sophisticated are not only said to be refined to the point of artificiality, but might well, because of this and despite their cleverness, be unsound.

Americans have for a long time shared the suspicion that sophisticated people, male or female, were somehow un-American. Open spaces and open people: that's what we've prided ourselves on. The good fellows, the regular guys, no nonsense about 'em, you know just where they stand; they look you in the eye and talk straight. As for sophisticated women, they're all right for a laugh or a show or a weekend, but who would want to marry 'em? No, sir, give me the girl next door every time, like home-baked pie.

Sophistication has always seemed something of an import, either from Europe or secondhand from New York. When women think of sophisticated men, their minds wander from British diplomats to French actors to Italian princes, settling in the end for those American men, mostly in movies, who have made love to British duchesses, French models, or Italian actresses.

European men possess a surface sophistication which may seem like the real thing even when it isn't. They kiss your hand with the proper lightness, and look into your eyes just long enough to create surface tension. Their voices are well modulated, and they do not rush you. They make a flattering show of savoring your intelligence, arriving at your body only at the dessert course of your first meal together. It is then that the tricks begin to show, to anyone, that is, not overcome by Chablis and long black lashes. They employ a standard routine that does not discriminate between you and a hundred other women, and is thus a product not of sophistication but of guile. It goes something like this: "You are beautiful, but you have not lived. Let me wake you. Only I can wake you. Most men want to take pleasure, I want to give it." Another very successful variation is the following gambit. European male: "How can you be so beautiful and so cold." Mary Jane from Wilmington: "I'm *not* cold." European male, whispering, breathing hard: "Then prove it to me."

If you prove it to him, you may have some pleasurable moments, but you'll discover before long that he is no more educated in world culture and the refinements of living than the agency man you met in Detroit, and probably less so. He has adopted a veneer of worldliness that passes for sophistication. Such common men have picked up some useful techniques. They know that an ardent look can be more effective than a hasty grab, and that masculine self-assurance is the best weapon against female resistance. By they are stereotypes for all that, while the mark of true sophistication is the absence of label.

As for our home-grown stereotypes, their approaches differ only in the crudity of their application, and the fact that too often they are impelled by liquor. I have never considered the amorous lurch a compliment, nor the mumbled repetition of endearments accompanied by uncertain groping. I am bored by a man so simple, so unsure, that he can approach a woman only by the chemical solvence of his inhibitions. I am dismayed by a man so unreticent that he can tell me about his wife and himself at our first encounter. This guilelessness, which is considered an American virtue, I find not only dull but immature. One of the joys of life is discovery, the gradual peeling of layers. It is a pity that society has accelerated this process to the degree of instant intimacy, or instimacy. Instead of a relished progression from *vous* to *tu,* it's "darling" and "come to my place" in the first hour. No. My sophisticated man does not tip his hand too soon.

You must have gathered from the foregoing that a sophisticated man likes women. I would go further and say that he prefers the company of women to men. He is not one for conventions or evenings with the boys. This does not mean that he does not relish conversations with men, but that given a social choice, he will favor the inclusion of women.

An appetite for experience would seem to make a sophisticated man less moral than our natural, open, simple man. Again, we return to the root of the old American-puritan distrust of him. Yet I maintain that the upstanding, regular, all-American male who marries the girl next door is really no more virtuous; he is merely less fastidious. It is he, on business trips, who patronizes call girls. The sophisticated man can gratify his desires without paying for them. It is our unsophisticated big-shot who uses his secretaries for more than typing; the wiser fellow keeps business and pleasure separate. It is our simple fellow who gets drunk and paws the high-school drum majorette. Our sophisticated man wouldn't be seen dead with her. The difference is that our regular guy has to prove his virility, while our sophisticated man exercises it quietly. He has long since abandoned proving for enjoying.

How a man lives, what he surrounds himself with, is index enough of his sophistication, or lack of it. There is nothing more revealing than a quiet prowl around his quarters. (I refer, of course, to bachelor quarters; a wife's contribution would complicate the issue.) Does he have flying geese over his mantel and the *Reader's Digest* on his coffee table? Are there no classics on his bookshelves? Does his record cabinet bulge with rock or jazz but lack Bach, Fauré or Prokofiev? Then prepare for a simple man and a limited one. His heart may be gold, but his company will be leaden.

I suspect, moreover, the too-neat room, for it can imply barrenness. The sophisticated man has many passions, and I salute them in a two-foot-pile of wide-ranging magazines on his desk, or in the unframed prints stacked on available ledges against the wall, awaiting hanging. I am also comforted by the presence in his kitchenette of hunks of cheese, some fruit, and a round loaf of bread, if nothing else. I suspect that his medicine cabinet may be rather full, for the price of sophistication is an awareness so constantly acute that it must be blunted from time to time. I would rather see a collection of pills, in short, than a rowing device.

I have omitted the lair of the bearded Zen-seeker and café poet, who is no more sophisticated than the glad-handing Shriner. He is merely less organized. They both abide by the conventions of their groups, their horizons equally limited by the exclusion of experience. There is in both the self-consciousness of the insecure. They live as they think they should, and it is not, thank heaven, with me.

I suspect that many women and more men may find my sophisticated man the portrait of an urban monster, effete, affected, immoral, snobbish, and unreliable. Urbane he certainly is, although I would put an appreciation of the natural world high in his category of perceptions. A man unaware or unmoved by sea or sky is not unsophisticated, he is merely half-alive. As for the imputed defects, I do not hold them as such. Instead of effete, I would say civilized; instead of affected, effective; instead of immoral, curious; instead of snobbish, superior.

As for unreliable, the sophisticated husband is more aware of the hazards and inconveniences of infidelity than the innocent one, if only because he has been married before.

DANCE-LOVER

You will find her at any evening of ballet and at most dance recitals. Her name is Lee, and she wears her thick, long, straight brown hair pulled back into a horsetail with elastic bands.

You will also recognize her by her sturdy, short, muscular body, and by the amount of crude leather she displays on her person: a wide calf's belt with coins set in it, a shoulder sack like a horse's feed bag, and sandals with a great many straps. In these her feet are planted almost defiantly. Her face is full-lipped and intense.

Lee is very passionate about dancing. It is her life. When she is not actually bending, stretching, leaping and squatting, she is looking at others leap and squat. When she is not looking, she is thinking of dancing, reading of dancing, dreaming of dancing.

This does not mean that she admires all kinds of dancing. Although conceding a certain technical proficiency, Lee finds classical ballet reactionary and frivolous. It is pretty (abhorrent quality) and means nothing. To Lee, everything must *mean something)*. The more tragic the meaning, the higher the art. That is why Lee is such a violent partisan of the abstract approach. There is not a movement of the body that does not mean something, usually of a pretty desperate nature.

Lee knows that the dance is far more than a bodily function. To be any good, it must spring from a richly cultivated mental and emotional soil. Lee's soil is composed of Kafka, Sartre, and agonized abstractionists in art and literature, notably the *Evergreen Review* and Jackson Pollock. The plot is wide enough to include Hieronymus Bosch and Henry Miller, but then the fence begins. In Lee's mind, nothing created before 1900 is any interest (except Bosch), and nothing lucid is of any importance. Only complexity has meaning. So when Lee recognizes an object in a painting, that damns the painter; and when she understands a line in a poem, that poet is representational and therefore lousy. As obscurity is a cherished quality in much of art, Lee is a happy girl.

In contrast to this, her moral concepts are surprisingly out of date. She believes in untrammeled sex as a free expression of personality. Lee dismisses monogamy as a delusion. She alarms most of the young men she knows with repeated hints at producing a baby. Illegitimately, of course. There would be no point in a legitimate one.

Next to embarrassing men, Lee finds deep enjoyment in embarrassing the government. This takes the form of agitating for immediate action when the government is either incapable of taking it, or engaged in delicate maneuvers to avoid it. The action would be fatal, but Lee is for it. She is currently picketing the consulate of an ally for motives which bear no relation to the actual facts, but which bear every relation to Lee's emotions.

Lee has a vocabulary all her own. It goes something like this: authority = dictatorship. Diplomat = fool. Patience = cowardice. Wisdom = inertia. Breeding = snobbishness. Charm = hyprocrisy. The past = reaction. Anyone who lives comfortably = a reactionary.

These definitions have one common denominator: innocence. Lee has never known authority, never met a diplomat, never had patience; lacks wisdom, possess no breeding; exerts no charm; is ignorant of the past, and lives uncomfortably.

In spite of this, Lee will probably develop into a very good dancer, of the school which defies the essence of the dance by never leaving the ground. As her center of gravity is very low, this is all for the best.

A NEW NIXON

See the new Nixon, so shining and sleek,
Push-button shifting and mirror veneer;
Notice the contour so simple and chic,
The silence of motor and absence of gear!

The bumpers are smaller, the chrome is reduced,
This is a model for every man's taste
But while you admire its powerful boost,
Watch for the brakes when the engine is raced.

SOME
PRACTICAL
EROTIC ADVICE

If I were a man, I'd be a rake until I married, and that, with any luck, would not be until my late twenties. I cannot imagine a better occupation of spare time than the seduction of a number of different women, unless, if you're a woman, it's seduction by a number of different men. It depends on how much vitality you have, and how fond you are of the opposite sex. I find the theory that this kind of sport is a sign of immaturity in men and disturbance in women rather preposterous. Many mature, productive, and distinguished men have trod the primrose path, and many wise women have, in their time, tasted the delights of compliance. How is one to recognize and practice virtue if one has not experienced its absence? What good is control if one has not endured the consequences of its lack?

The Church and psychiatry have done their best to discredit dilatory passions, which is why most American men have a limited understanding of women, and most American women have suffered from this ignorance. The domesticated male may be safe, but he is not exciting.

When I married, after my explorations, I would prefer as my life partner, if I were a man, a woman who knew almost as much as I did. I say almost, because men like to teach, and think they have the edge of experience.

All great lovers are articulate, and verbal seduction is the surest road to actual seduction. The man who knows this can prevail over a handsomer, tongue-tied rival. Young men can afford to be speechless blunderers, but if they want to exert attraction in later years, they had better learn to talk.

And I do not mean garrulity. I mean talk directly addressed to the woman *about* the woman. Verbal attention is as important as sexual attention. It is the knowledge of what to say, when.

It is also the knowledge of every facet of the woman herself, which must be reflected back to her in words. For the woman, to love a man, must be in love with herself as *he* sees her. This is mutual narcissism, but I think it is stronger in women than in men, and more demanding. General compliments are pleasing to hear, but the specific, targeted endearment bears far greater fruit. For the man who remarks on the line of her chin or the shape of her thigh, a woman will do anything. They don't tell you this in the sex manuals.

Another heresy. If I were a man, having won a woman, I think that I would be tough with her, exacting deference to my masculinity and rebuffing aggressive inroads of all kinds. I would not tolerate the loud or derisive voice, or any efforts, private or public, to diminish my stature as a man. I would exert this dominance because women expect and want it, and when they don't get it, they are left with contempt for the man.

If I were a man, I would be a hellion.

KEEP OUT
THE AIR

Look at any window in any house in any town in the United
States, and what do you see? The half-lowered shade or blind. Why?
So that the sun will not fade the fabrics? Today's fabrics do not fade,
and besides, the sun never enters half of these windows. Privacy?
The lower half of the window is unshielded, and in any case what do
a wholly gregarious people want with privacy? Gentility? Whose
gentility? And why is it genteel to admit only half the available light?

This half-shade, you can plainly see, has become an obsession;
unconscious in the nation, conscious in me. I do not know the reason
for it, but I think I see a meaning in it. It is a fear of exposure in the
deepest sense. Three hundred years ago it may have been as simple
as a fear of the outer wilderness, a need to shutter out the dangerous
night and shutter in the small, close world of man. I can understand
the shade drawn wholly against the unknown, but why half against
the known?

I think the half-drawn blind is still part of a general fear of the
elements, in particular of light and air. In diminishing the effects of
weather, we have diminished our resistance to it.

A greater part of our people live without air all day long, and
muffle their children up to the ears in airtight clothes at the first hint
of cold. Women in fur coats shop in stores too hot for salesgirls in
silks. The fear of cold leaves the park empty on days when sun and
wind make it beautiful; days when a park in Europe is full of children
playing and people walking. And rain? Who walks in rain except to
the nearest shelter?

Americans are so protected by the marvels of their technology
that their bundled children succumb to every bug, their adolescent
boys have nightclub pallor and smokers' chests (the girls go better:

150

vanity saves them), and too many men and women suffer the chronic twin fatigues of anoxia and inertia from a life without air and adequate movement.

Is it then any wonder that telephone linemen, oil drillers, cow hands and forest rangers are the best-looking men in the land?

I recommend the construction of committees where men and women would walk to work and the children to school. Where boys would not be permitted to drive cars until they were twenty. Where health authorities would regulate the temperatures of public places to a level best for public health. Where every healthy citizen would have a period of mandatory daily exposure to whatever weather existed, however bad. I would also like to see one day a week when all facilities were suspended: light, heat, gas and water. We might then learn an independence which could teach us an ultimate survival. Rigor is a good governess.

When nature is overridden, she takes her revenge. Though science has lengthened our span, it may have weakened our fiber. If nature cannot harm us, neither can she endow us now with her strength. We have put up all sorts of shields against her reality, and the half-drawn shade is one of them. It is one more evasion of truth, a word which, in our present vocabulary, is synonymous with discomfort. So we temper the brilliance of light and the sting of air, stewing in our own juice.

"HAVEN'T YOU
LOST WEIGHT
DEAR?"

If American men are obsessed with money, American women are obsessed with weight. The men talk of gain, the women talk of loss, and I do not know which talk is the more boring.

The first thing a woman looks at in another woman is her waistline. The first salutation is, "You're a little thinner, aren't you?" Or, "Haven't you been putting on a little weight, dear?" The first is the ultimate compliment, the second is the ultimate insult. I consider both bad taste, since they are no business of the speaker's. A woman's shape and size is entirely her affair, and if she's happy and hippy she should be left alone. Some of art's greatest nudes have been fleshy, wide, and beautiful, and I am willing to wager that their radiance was the reflection of masculine appreciation. It is only fairly recently that men are supposed to prefer the bony splendors of the pelvic cradle.

I am not defending obesity, nor doubting the beauty of a slim young body. I do take issue with the prevailing conviction that there is only one acceptable feminine outline for all ages of her life, which, if you except the grotesque mammalian exaggerations of certain film stars, is basically rectilinear, as in a pipe, and that no beauty of face, excitement of mind, or warmth of spirit can excuse or nullify the sin of a widened posterior.

The result is apparent: a race of women far thinner than their mothers at their age, and considerably younger in appearance up to the face. There you see the price paid in tension, harassment, and preoccupation. There is nothing relaxing about this kind of fight.

Mass production of clothes depends on the simplest cut and the least fabric. This, in turn, can be worn only by the thin. It has

THE BEST OF MARYA MANNES   153

become impossible for a woman who is not rich to dress properly if she does not fall within the dimensions of a slender girl of sixteen.

If she cannot diet or exercise or otherwise force herself within these, she is lost to fashion. Any woman familiar with clothes in the "larger sizes" knows what this means. They are the shrouds of sex, the sacraments of abdication. If you have to get into these, they seem to say, you might as well give up; *we* have.

Now this is nonsense. There is no reason why a woman who is heavier or broader than this adolescent "ideal" cannot be dressed both fashionably and seductively. Designers and dress manufacturers could see to this if they wanted to, but it would militate against the hucksters of exercise, the slenderizing salons, fat farms, and pill-producers of the nation. For then a woman could be attractive without their help, and that would never do.

No, by heaven, whittle her down to size. Their size. And devil take her pocketbook and her peace of mind. For this dubious praise, "Haven't you lost a little weight, dear?," she sacrifices one of the greatest pleasures of life, the eating of good food. To anyone who appreciates this delight, the sight of a woman declining a fine cream sauce, a baked potato, or a crême brulée is more displeasing than admirable, and also insulting to the cook. I am sure that a man's pleasure in asking a woman to dinner is diminished by this self-serving abstinence. He might, if given the chance, settle for a few more pounds and a little more gusto. Unless, of course, he is the kind of man, and there are some, who prefer mannequins to woman; in which case he isn't worth bothering about in the first place.

So relax, you women tyrannized by tape measures and scales. Have fun, eat well, and be kind to your fellows. And the next time a woman remarks on your weight, tell her what she can do with it.

THE LANSINGS
AND THE KAPPELS

There are so many reasons to live on Park Avenue, good and bad. If I were asked to describe typical Park Avenue apartments, I would concentrate on two particular kinds. One would be the home of a Social Register kind of family, and the other would belong, say, to the president of a chain of department stores.

Let us visit George and Amy Lansing first. George is an investment banker with a Wall Street firm; Amy is the daughter of a prominent corporation lawyer, lately deceased. George's family has lived in Glens Falls for five generations, Amy's ancestors fought the Revolution in Virginia. They have a daughter at Brearley, a son at Yale, and a house at Stockbridge, used on weekends and summer vacations. George is on many boards, Amy on many charities. Their large rooms are carpeted wall-to-wall in a neutral shade, the sofas and chairs are covered either in flowered muted chintz or beige brocade, and the curtains drawn across the windows are of matching chintz. The furniture is mostly English antique. Over the fireplace is a portrait, thinly painted, of Amy's mother, the kind of woman with the long, sloping, undivided bust mysteriously achieved in her day, and an expression of mild reproof. The other pictures are mostly etchings of ducks in flight or English hunting prints, and the tops of tables are crowded with family photographs in silver frames. There is nothing in the rooms that could possibly offend anyone and nothing that could possibly delight. The Lansings have comfort for their money but no fun, and the observant guest cannot help but pity such spiritual constipation. What is more, two sets of curtains and a half-lowered shade cut out in daytime the luxury of light that their fifteenth-floor apartment could provide them, and this perpetual muffling and diffusion, carpeting and covering gives these rooms the feeling of large and elaborate padded cells in which one could die of anoxia. Physically and mentally, the Lansings are sealed in their own amber.

This is never more apparent than at one of their cocktail parties. For they invite themselves: pleasant, easy, handsome people from the world of law or finance, usually Republican, always well-groomed, and always well-mannered. One searches in vain for an expressive, an unguarded, or even an ugly face. At the Lansings you will see no Jews, no artists, no musicians, no eccentrics, and only those foreigners, usually from the north of Europe, who could be taken, except for their accents, for Americans or Englishmen of the Lansings' class. No voice is raised there except in joviality, no alien note intrudes, no new thought penetrates to surprise or disturb. All in all, the Lansing living room is the social equivalent of that experiment in weightlessness and the absence of sensory reflexes in which a man is suspended in tepid water: there is nothing to move against or measure against.

The Kappels, a few blocks north, are very different in certain ways. For one thing, Joseph Kappel's grandparents emigrated from Europe in the middle of the nineteenth century, and Liz is a born New Yorker of Midwestern stock. For another, Joe started fairly humbly as a small importer of fabrics and in twenty years amassed a chain of high-class department stores in New York and the suburbs.

In their apartment, they show it chiefly through the taste of Robin, a much-sought-after Fifty-seventh Street decorator who changes their rooms at intervals to keep pace with fashion. Fifteen years ago, Robin persuaded the Kappels to go whole hog on French Impressionsists, and Joe acquired a rather muddy little Renoir head, a weak Bonnard, a Seurat sketch for *La Grande jatte,* a Degas etching (the laundress), and a very blurry Monet. To complement these, Robin bought them the most expensive examples of French provincial furniture that he could find in Europe, and keyed the upholstery with infinite subtlety to their tones.

But last year a revolution took place. Joe took the Impressionists to his office (where they impressed), and Robin made over the Kappel home to accommodate a Baziotes, a de Kooning, a Dubuffet, a Franz Kline, and a metal construction composed of pipes and fender strips called *Birdwatcher*. All these required white walls, the severest contemporary furniture (including several couches that suggest upholstered mortuary slabs), and the occasional bright jab of an orange, black, or acid-pink pillow. An extra ceiling was suspended, above which invisible fixtures cast diffused light and gave the faces of Kappels and guests the look of recent exhumation. It was quite a room. Only when Liz took women guests to her boudoir did her interior struggle (lost to Robin except in this sanctuary) become apparent. An Edzard pastel of a wistful young girl in a ribboned bonnet hung over her frilled and canopied bed, and every white shelf in this pink-lined box was crammed with bibelots: round, colored paperweights, white milk glasses, and porcelain hands in every position needed to hold nuts, ashes, or a single rose, although never put to these uses.

Although the Kappels have a few close friends from former days to whom they are loyal, and dinners for business associates are given from time to time, their parties are usually reserved for celebrities they know only slightly. Having backed a few Broadway hits, they have access to people of the theater, and Robin has seen to it that the Kappels keep in touch with current newsmakers in the world of art, provided they are socially housebroken. As few of the most prominent contemporary painters qualify, the guests are likely to be museum curators, collectors, critics, and fashion photographers, who give ecstatic sanction to the Kappels' taste but pose no threat to their marriage.

Few would doubt, however, that the Kappel parties were more amusing than the Lansing ones. The major difference between these two family residents of Park Avenue is that the Lansings have roots and the Kappels have none. George and Amy are secure in their past, Joe and Liz are insecure in their present. And while the Lansings accept Park Avenue as a matter of course in their way of

living, the Kappels remind themselves of their position every time
the doorman greets them.

THE RUBAIYAT
OF OMAR HILTON

*Now, in 1963, the minarets
of Iran and the Acropolis of
Greece look out on two wonders of
the modern world...History
meets tomorrow with two new
Hilton Hotels—Adv.*

The moving Builder builds, and having built
Moves on; the Milk (or rather Concrete) split,
  The kinship claimed with an offended Past
That watches Profit grow and Beauty wilt.

Yesterday this day's Madness did prepare:
Tomorrow's Hostel and the People there,
  Who may know Whence they came but hardly Why—
Except to Drink and Sleep and Sit and Stare.

A moment's Halt, a momentary Taste
Of Culture from the Well among the Waste,
  And lo—the tourist Caravan has reached
The Nothing it set out from, Hilton-based.

ROBIN'S WORLD

The women who visit Robin's apartment are inclined to wonder why men ever bother to marry. They live so much more comfortably alone. Robin's place is perfection, a garden duplex in the East Sixties furnished in exquisite taste in a mixture of Regency and modern, run by a pale and graceful black, animated by a huge and uncannily sensitive brown poodle, and free of such blurring traces of feminine presence as stockings drying in the bathroom and a clutter of jars. Even the canapés are better than the ones served in homes of the married.

Robin, moreover, appears to be exempt from those devotions, obligations, and incubi which make other people tired, old and cross, harried, debt-ridden, and dull. If he has aging parents, they are never seen; being unmarried, he has neither children nor parents-in-law; old friends who are dull are friends no more; and even cousins seem not to exist. Since he has no one to support, the sums that he earns through his thriving business of interior decoration are spent on a way of life entirely pleasing to himself. And it must be admitted that Robin is an artist in pleasure, choosing only those objects, colors, sounds, and textures which flatter the senses, excluding those which offend or enervate. The exclamation of delight uttered by a new visitor gives Robin a sense of altruism dispelling any faint twinge (the twinges are fainter every year) of remorse at what some people have called his selfish life. He gives pleasure freely to others; if they are so transported by his taste as to demand his professional services, well, that is their concern. He did not force them into it.

Robin has other attributes beside taste. He is quite decorative, in a fluid way, and very funny. He has a pronounced gift for mimicry, and it is generally felt that he could have adorned the theater.

There is, in fact, no field of creative effort in which Robin is not entirely at home. His cocktail parties and little buffets are likely to include the most successful photographers, painters, choreographers, composers, film directors, and writers in town, and certainly the leaders in the world of fashion. No fashion editor worth her salt fails to know Robin and count him as her friend, and his decors and the works of his companions are responsible for her most spectacular pages. It might be said that Robin's circle *is* the fashion.

It is a tightly closed society, this circle: a light and airy *cénacle* of the arts, or if you prefer, an Old Pals' Act rigid in its dedication and loyalty. The larger society is split into smaller cells: painter, art critic, dealer; screenwriter, film critic, director; composer, music critic, performer; dancer, choreographer, manager; writer, editor, publisher, and so forth. Around these seperate cells is a chorus of young men and older women, a galaxy of the rootless, there to applaud, to cosset, to crown. It is the rare artist who succeeds without belonging to Robin's world.

Robin and his companions have many talents but little love, except for these talents and for each other, and theirs is a love that leads inward. They love their love of beauty, they love their sensibilities, and they love their persons. With great attention they keep supple and slim, offering their skin as often as they can to the golden approval of the sun. For this purpose, they claim the best beaches and the best coasts in the world, from Fire Island to Barbados, from Morocco to Corsica. When these beaches are ultimately found and claimed by the vulgar, they move to others more distant, more concealed. Stumble upon a beautiful hidden cove and Robin will be there sunning, his russet or mahogany towel beside him, and the poodle, Flaubert, bounding at the waves.

Yet the gaiety, the ease, and the brilliance that characterize the world of Robin do not preclude a netherworld, darker than one might suppose and inhabited by things that are not pretty. Spite, jealousy, rage, revenge, these plague Robin's society. The energies others expend on supporting wives, raising families, monotony, or privation are here diverted into intense and exclusive relationships. When these are harmonious, all is perfect. When they sour, hell is unleashed. The one found guilty of the breach becomes quite suddenly the object of bad reviews, for the sweetest ostracism in this circle is professional, and the course of personal relationships can be quite easily followed in the critical press.

Over or beneath it all, this exquisite, tasteful, witty, and powerful stratum, is a profound discontent that neither Robin nor his friends ever allow themselves to admit, for they consider themselves in nearly all ways superior to their fellows. They are, for all their success, not in the mainstream of life, for the one quality absent in their world is humanity.

Yet humanity might blur their judgment, might impel them, out of affection or pity, to accept a failure, a talent out of its time, an embarrassment. And this no arbiter of taste can afford to do.

SUMMER
THOUGHTS
OF A SNOB

Now that the Off is Beaten Track, preserve me from
Summer in Europe. I have no wish to go
Where the rest are going: Bill, Edie, Ed, the man who does my hair

Miss P. in Filing, the Marches with their young,
The folk from Winnetka, Purple Springs, Wahooskie,
A million Americans bound for the lovely places
I once saw hearing only a different tongue and seeing
Strange people and smelling and tasting newly every day.
Strange to myself as well as strange to others.

Preserve me now
From a Europe tailored to our aseptic tastes, with Haig and Haig
Handy in every wineshop in every province
And Cokes all over; and in some mountain town
Drene, Gleem and Kleenex, Pond's, Band-Aid and Lux
Ready on shelves for timid modern women,
And every village geared to childish lips
With franks and hamburgers and banana splits
Where cheese and wine once warmed the exploring tongue.

Preserve me from One World, One Way, Our Way
Prevailing, the common coinage of the kingdom of comfort
Dispelling difference. And save me from seeing
David in Florence surrounded by my kind,
However happy, humble, decent and generous:

The rumpled men, shirts open, the straps of gear
Dragging their Dacron shoulders down, their slackened mouths
Loose-hung. Preserve me from their wives,
Eager in cottons, pixie-glasses bright,
Telling their families shrilly where to look.
Preserve me from their young—the pretty, precocious
Girls, kid-brother boys
Fat-buttocked in their jeans, the slouching youths
Looking for Bardot, bored with Bargello.

Preserve me too
From all my sophisticated friends who know just where
To eat, sleep, drive, buy charming little things
At next to nothing. Let them go, I say,
And blessings on them for all the joys they reap.
I will stay here. The places in their season
Are for too many. Antibes, the Costa Brava,
Rome, Venice, Capri, Ischia, all those places
Eye-worn, herd-trodden, overused, un-strange,
Vacation-weary. I do not want those beaches
Padded with basting flesh, the *trattorias*
Loud with American cries, while waiters' eyes
Glisten derisively, their palms outstretched
For the preposterous overtip.

Preserve me too
From the Germans and English in Italy and France
And the French in France, high-voiced in penury
On their paid holidays. All men are equal
To see all things, and this is fine for them, but I
Prefer the priority of singleness
In seeing. To be the one
Stranger before the undiscovered sight, the house or hill
None else is seeing now. And if this means

Choosing the bitter climates of the year,
The shrouded sun, cold rooms, deserted streets,

And worst of all, places still poor in plumbing—
Tell no one else; but I, a snob,
Am coming.

THE
CREATIVE
WOMAN

Many times during this examination of a certain kind of woman and the world she lives in, I have asked myself, who cares? You and I have read scores of articles in these last years about the great wasted reservoir of female intelligence, about the nation's need not only for educated women but for thinking women, trained and ready to apply their skills in professions that presumably cry out for them. If the call is there, I have not heard it. And if the need is there, society, including women, either ignores it or rejects it.

The only reason that I am adding words to this subject is to clear away what I consider to be a thicket of misconceptions and timidities. Some of my ideas, therefore, are bound to be unpalatable to many of our citizens who believe that prosperity and procreation, in wedlock, of course, are the only valid goals of man and woman. I happen to think that there are other goals as valid, and valuable.

How did I get that way? Well, I saw it around me when I was a small child. My mother and father were both concert musicians and both teachers, my mother of the piano, my father of the violin. There was nothing strange for me in the fact that my mother spent much of the day practicing or giving lessons, that she went off on tour with my father, and that she couldn't boil an egg. She didn't have to. In the early part of the twentieth century, even people of very modest means had cooks and nurses, and it was taken equally for granted by my brother and myself that if our mother was away, the cook, the nurse, or the great-aunt who lived with us, would take care of us. There was no sense of rejection, no shocks at being motherless for a period of weeks. Life went on fully; we studied, ate, and slept, and when our parents did come back, we were delighted to see them.

Now you can say two things that I, as a child, did not then realize. One was that my mother was an exceptional woman. the other was that servants and relatives made it possible for her to maintain a professional life and a domestic life without harm to either. Both were true. I can add one more thing: that the temper of the time was different. The mass media had not enthroned the housewife as God's noblest creature and best consumer, reams of nonsense were not being written about woman's proper role, and women themselves did not regard the minority of professional or career women with a mixture of envy, disapproval, and superiority.

I grew up believing that all was possible for a girl or a woman. Certainly both my father and my brother made it seem so. Both spoke to me as equals of many things that girls are not supposed to be interested in. My brother passed on the first principles of physics, the relativity of time, and how to throw a curve with a baseball. My father discussed with me, from the age of ten years onward, such things as the nature of melancholy, how to get a vibrato on a violin, and how sickness could be caused by states of mind. I lived for over seventeen years in a world of imagination and discovery, going steady not with the boy next door but the men out of range. My lovers included Julius Caesar, Hamlet, Henry V, and John Barrymore. I did not start transferring my affections to more attainable men until I was nineteen, at which point I threw away the books, along with self-restraint.

But at no time, then or since, did I throw away a sense of fierce independence as a human being, and the desire to attain distinction in terms of mind and spirit and expression.

I have dwelt on this background not because it was right for a woman or natural for a woman, but because it was right and natural for the kind of human being that I happen to be. Each person, male or female, is composed of both male and female components that vary in proportion according to the individual. Yet this generally acknowledged complexity of roles, the result of a long, slow, dramatic sexual revolution, has been consciously rejected by the public in many quarters. Why? Because it challenges the whole structure of marriage, the family, society as we know it now. It challenges a good many timeworn assumptions that have been not only comfortable for men but convenient for the majority of women, too.

Equality is not an issue here. What is at issue is the recognition of minorities, among which creative women and nonaggressive men are the largest. By nonaggressive men, I mean those who are uncompetitive: the dreamers rather than the doers, the non-go-getters, sensitive and gentle men. Equipped neither as fighters nor, primarily, as breadwinners, lacking the desire to impose their will on others or to dominate the women they love, they are as valuable as their macho brothers.

That this recognition must extend to and include homosexuals at either end of the spectrum goes without saying. They exist, they are here, they will not go away. The point is to make them productive, to recognize the values they have, to incorporate them openly and without prejudice into our society. For it is the refusal to accept and even value their differences from the norm that causes harm: the problems which I am here confining to the creative woman.

What exactly are these problems? The earliest are her parents. From infancy they give her no choice to be anything but what they think a girl should be. They smother her in pink when she might prefer blue. They give her dolls when she might prefer trains. They proffer books about girls when she might rather read about boys, and they send her to a psychiatrist if she, at sixteen, likes books better than boys. They initiate the mating process when she is twelve, in the firm conviction that the only possible future for her is early marriage, lots of children, and a suburban home. If their girl shows a desire to paint or model or write verse, the more intelligent parents encourage her. A talent is fine so long as it is kept within bounds, meaning the existing horizons and biases of her parents.

Even if her parents are proud of her intellectual curiosity, her talent, her independence of spirit, she can never escape the relentless nudging of society: the assumption that she is in some way unfeminine, that she is jeopardizing her future happiness as a woman, that what she is doing is merely a substitute for her true (and only valid) functions. She sees ahead of her an entire generation of women, home-bound and house-oriented to a degree not even experienced by their own mothers, and certainly not dreamed of by those valiant pioneers of sixty years ago whose militant efforts to widen women's horizons and take them *out* of the kitchen earned them ridicule as well as rights. They must be turning in their graves to see many of their female descendants, blessed today with home computers, micro-wave ovens, every possible device to use time well, not only being full-time servants to their husbands and children, but serene on their sense of superiority over their career-bound sisters.

So our girl in this free country has, in truth, little choice. Security is the goal, and as soon as possible. Now what is wrong with that, you say? The majority of women have found their greatest fulfillment in the home, as wife and mother. Why grudge them their happiness just because it isn't yours?

I do not grudge them their happiness. I merely question whether in a more fluid society they might not make better doctors than mothers, better mathematicians than homemakers, better courtesans than wives. I could question equally whether the young men trapped into domesticity and corporations in their early twenties would not be happier as explorers than fathers, poets than husbands, and rakes than lawnmowers.

Society accepts the creative woman only on certain conditions. It is her attempt to gain this acceptance by fulfilling these conditions that makes for trouble.

No one objects to a woman being a good writer or sculptor or geneticist if at the same time she manages to be a good wife, mother, etc. This is the entrance charge for the approval of other men and women, and I think that it is exorbitant to the point of impossibility. Nobody expected George Eliot to be a beauty. Emily Dickinson was not scorned for being childless. Nobody urged Marie Curie to dye her hair.

Beauty is possibly the greatest hazard of a creative woman. Male adoration is a powerful deterrent to female sense, and it is extremely difficult to tear one's self from loving arms and say, "Sorry, darling, I've got to work." It is so much easier and pleasanter to drown in current delights than gird for future dreams. We try to have both, of course, but the split is there to stay, if you think a certain way.

If she is worried about what others think of her, by what standards of morality she is judged, she will not stand the gaff of independence long. If the creative woman marries and has children, her life will be divided three ways between her children, her husband, and her work. What she gives to one, she must take from the other. In this, as in many other things, the creative woman has a tougher time than the creative man. For all of our vaunted modernity, not enough people believe that her time is sacred. A man at his desk in a room with a closed door is a man at work. A woman at a desk in any room is available.

ON FITNESS
AND SENIORITY
IN CONGRESS

Let's have a committee of cats
To rule on the rights of mice;

Let's have a committee of poets
To give the kettles advice;

The devil examines sin,
The blemished exonerate taint;

If you're old enough, you're in;
If you're honest enough, you ain't.

DEAR MUMMY

Mrs. Howard Andrews
Our Place
Crestview, Ohio

Dear Addie,

Your father and I are very disturbed about something we just heard from the Maitlands (they came aboard yesterday for drinks). Ginny said that just before they left for Flat Key, Ann Rossiter called her from Oakdale and said that the Westover girl had given a birthday party that turned into something of a riot. She was very vague about the details, but it seems things got very rough and the house was a shambles. We are very worried because we remember that Doug had been seeing something of the Westover girl, and we naturally hope he wasn't involved.

Please let us know what, if anything, happened.

Love,
Mummy

Mr. and Mrs. Curtis Munson
Fool's Paradise
Flat Key, Bahamas

Dearest Mummy,

It's just like Ginny Maitland to go gabbing away like that, upsetting people for no reason. We are all trying to keep the affair in the family, so to speak, and Howie even saw to it that Ed Bates didn't print anything about it in the Oakdale *Sentinel.* Franny Westover *did* give a birthday party for about a hundred kids, and I guess it went on a little late and the boys wanted some fun and threw a few things around. Doug doesn't seem to remember exactly what happened. Apparently someone thought it would be funny if they had a "book-wetting" and threw all of the books from the house into the swimming pool, and then someone else (I think it was a girl) thought that it would be fun to have everyone take off their ordinary clothes and dress in window curtains.

Dick Westover was very unpleasant over the phone yesterday (we never liked him anyway) and accused Doug of being one of the boys who cut up the living-room rug with pruning shears, but it was a hideous mustard broadloom (that house is in the *worst* taste) and I don't much blame them.

The point is, Daddy, it was a simple case of high spirits and no real harm done. I gave Doug a check for $3,000 to cover some glassware and the rug business (he swears he didn't burn any curtains).

So please don't worry about it. Doug is a fine boy, really, and those were the nicest kids anyone would want to know, all from the best homes and Yale and Princeton and all that.

Love and Kisses,
Addie

Mrs. Howard Andrews
Our Place
Crestview, Ohio

Dear *Addie*,

Your father had one of his attacks of indigestion after getting your letter, and has asked me to write you.

I need hardly say we were appalled. How is it possible for boys of decent families to destroy the property of other people who are giving them a party? In my day, the parents and older people were always around.

Your Distressed Mother,
Mother

P.S. If I'd been you and Howie, I'd have made Doug pay for the damage out of his own pocket and taken away his college tuition for a semester. How else will these spoiled young ruffians ever learn?

Dad

Mrs. Curtis Munson
Fool's Paradise
Andros, Bahamas

Dear Mummy,
Your letter shows how out of touch you two have been with things today. No self-respecting parent would *dream* of being in the house when the kids are having a party, it inhibits them so. Howie and I just engage the band and the caterer and have our own fun somewhere else. Just to be on the safe side, we did hire a policeman for Carol's last party, to see that crashers didn't get out-of-hand. In case you didn't know, it's the custom for a lot of kids to drive to a party they haven't been invited to, and in a way I think it's very democratic even if they do make a sort of mess of the place. But we always get a house-cleaning crew in the next day to sweep up the broken glass, refinish the furniture, and plant new bushes. It's just part of the expense of entertaining these days.

Also, I don't see how you can say that Doug is spoiled. He deserved a turbocharged sports car for getting into Yale (Howie never thought he'd make it), and as for his new speedboat this summer, well, you couldn't really expect him to take his dates across the lake in an outboard.

Doug is not a ruffian. Why only the other day, Mr. Ballard (he's Vice President of Western Swivel) told Howie that Doug was a natural leader with a real feeling for money.

Love,
Addie

Mrs. Howard Andrews
Our Place
Crestview, Ohio

Dear Addie,

"Natural leaders with a real feeling for money" have been known to land in jail. Doug may too, someday, if you and Howie don't set him straight before it's too late.

Speaking of which, have you ever bothered to tell the kid about right and wrong and responsibility? Where's his father been all of this time? How can you possibly expect kids who drink hard liquor from fourteen on and crash parties and need policemen to keep them in order to turn into decent citizens?

High spirits my hat. Those boys need a flogging or a psychiatric examination. Not that I believe in that stuff, it's mostly mumbo-jumbo, but something must be wrong inside if a boy has to destroy something to feel good.

Love,
Dad

Mrs. Curtis Munson
Fool's Paradise
Eleuthera, Bahamas

Dear Mummy,
I can't write to Dad in his present condition. He just doesn't understand the realities of today.

For one thing, Doug went to Sunday School from the ages of 8 to 10, and then at prep school they had the Lord's Prayer every morning before they banned it. So he's had as good a Christian upbringing as anyone.

For another, Dad seems to forget that when Doug was fifteen, he won the D.A.R. prize for the best essay on Why Our Way of Life Is the Best Way. So don't talk to me about ethics.

And what does Dad mean asking where Howie's been? Howie's in town every day as he well knows, working so that we can have a decent standard of living, and it isn't his fault that he doesn't see his son from one end of the week to the other. It's the mother's responsibility anyway, and God knows I've given Doug everything since he was a tiny baby.

What Dad refuses to realize is that it's terribly hard growing up with the bomb and insecurity. Boys like Doug don't know what's going to happen to them, so they have to have some outlet somewhere.

Love,
Addie

Telegram to Mrs. Howard Andrews:
RE OUTLET HOW ABOUT HONEST WORK OR THE
PEACE CORPS?

DAD

Mr. Curtis Munson
Fool's Paradise
St. James, Barbados

Dear Curtis,
Addie has just showed me your letter and telegram, and as she is rather emotional about all this, I thought I'd write to you directly.
My personal view is that the Communists are behind all those so-called riots you read about. I don't doubt that some Harvard pinko got into that Westover party and planted the whole thing so that it would reflect badly on our society.
Anyway, you have no cause to worry about Doug. He's a fine, red-blooded kid with a great sense of humor and a lot of git-up-an-go. What it all comes down to is, what would you rather have: a free society or a socialist state?

Cordially,
Howie

Miss Frances Westover
Oakdale, Ohio

Dear Fran,
I'm sorry you thought I sounded mad when you phoned me the news yesterday, but you can understand why it was something of a shock, especially as I don't remember a thing that happened that night, any more than you did. Somebody shot the lights out and I couldn't see who the hell I was with.
Honest, I'm glad it was you, and we might as well have a family now as later anyway.
I'll break the news to my old lady next weekend. It'll take her mind off this price-fixing, and Dad's company you've probably read about. Anyway, relax. I'll be calling you.

Your everlovin' Doug

Mr. and Mrs. Curtis Munson
Fool's Paradise
Tobago, Trinidad

Dear Dad and Mom,
I know you'll be as happy as I am to know that Doug is engaged to
Frances Westover and they hope to be married very soon. She's a
darling girl (they're Mainland Steel), and they seem in a romantic
daze about each other. So you see, little Doug who worried you so is
now about to become a responsible married man and, of course,
some day, the father of a family.
I am hoping that after he finishes college (Howie naturally will see
them through that), they'll settle somewhere near us so that the
children can grow up in a fine healthy community with people who
think alike and have the same values.
Doug will write to you himself, I know. In spite of his sometimes
casual manner, he is really very fond of you both, even if the
generations don't always mix. Young people are more realistic, don't
you think?

Lovingly,
Addie

THE CONFESSION
OF MARK GUTZLER

TO: The United States Advisory Board for Literary Excellence (USABLE).

After the public chastisement so rightly administered to me by USABLE, I must apologize to your distinguished body and the American people for any and all unwitting deviations I have made from the true direction of American writing, as established by those who decide what is good and what is bad in this country.

With a heavy heart and a cleansed spirit, I accept the new critical standards of the day and confess to the following sins against literary worth as defined by USABLE.

The first sin was committed by my parents, who failed to belong to an oppressed minority, who lived in middle-class comfort in an urban section without literary value, being neither in slum nor ghetto, and neither in the South nor the Middle West. It has been a source of continuing anguish to me that their life, if indeed it can be called such, produced none of the festering hatreds which alone give experience. USABLE has rightly accused me of writing that some persons are good, or noble. I know now that this is not so, and that we are all equally vile.

My parents were responsible also for the fact that my adolescence was neither particularly painful nor confused. I remember being very happy fishing alone, mountain climbing, and cataloguing rock specimens. I also played the flute, an offensively pure instrument. None of this, I now see, is suitable background for a serious writer.

I further confess with shame to a long apprenticeship in the art and craft of writing. That this was a weakening and perverting experience I now, to my sorrow, admit. To quote USABLE's indictment: "Knowledge of the structure and use of language can produce a graceful style wholly incongruous to the realities of the present, and, what is worse, can give the reader a simple pleasure incompatible with the recognition of true art." I was led astray in my youth by the sinful love of words and a slavish attention to the so-called masters of literature in the past. My writing has therefore been sapped of the qualities of accident and error that give strength and importance to the best of contemporary writing. In a misguided attempt to communicate clearly to others, I have sacrificed that priceless ingredient of true talent: obscurity. As USABLE stated, clarity bears the stigma of order. The true writer reflects chaos.

In the future I will make comprehension as difficult as possible in the hopes of being praised by the critics, if not read by the public.

Of all USABLE's charges against me, the most serious is the use of restraint and moderation, the result of cowardice, and worse, of taste. A thorough examination of my collected writings revealed only six four-letter words and two consummations of the sex act. Concerning the latter, the examiners noted grave omissions of detail that were subsequently filed under the heading "Evasion of Reality." My pitifully meager lot was to have been educated in sex by a pleasant older woman, and to have been married to the same wife for fifteen years. In my own defense, however, I must state categorically that I am very fond of liquor and have been known to pass out on various occasions, one of them particularly disgusting.

The omission of clinical sexual detail in my works has been due to a belief, mistaken, I now know, that something should be left to the imagination of the reader. USABLE's strictures have made me realize that this is a public disservice, since what the reader imagines is worse than any reality and therefore potentially more damaging, psychologically and emotionally, than the printed word.

It may interest USABLE to learn that my next book will concern the adventures of two midgets, one fund raiser, three dictators, and fourteen whores working in an imaginary Alliance for Progress. I have no idea how it will come out.

Against USABLE's final charge: that, since no writer more

than forty years old can presume to be hailed as a "talent," I have no literary future, I can muster no defense. It is quite understandable that important critics concern themselves more with promise than performance, since praise of the former is less onerous than judgment of the latter. My new book, *Naked Belch,* promises to be very promising.

In conclusion, I wish to thank the United States Advisory Board for Literary Excellence for showing me my grievous errors and lighting a new path toward creative value. I am a new man, and a new writer.

Humbly yours,

MARK GUTZLER
(formerly known as Marya Mannes)

BEE LINE

*Congress was told today that it is danger-
ous for American honeybees to associate
with foreign honeybees.*

Ah love, how
sweet
To pollinate
Across the sea!

Your foreign fuzz
And alien buzz
Enchanted me!

But now it seems
Our honeyed
dreams
Can be no more—

A cruel state
Decrees I mate
The bee next door

WHAT'S WRONG
WITH OUR PRESS?

(A SPEECH)
Reprinted in
The Reporter,
May 12, 1960.

Newspapers have two great advantages over television. They can be used by men as barriers against their wives. It is still the only effective screen against the morning features of the loved one, and, as such, performs a uniquely human service. The second advantage is that you can't line a garbage pail with a television set. It's usually the other way around.

The fact is that although network television still allots too little time to the vital service of informing the public, it does a better job in that little time than the nation's press as a whole. And when I speak of the nation's press as a whole, I am *not* referring to five or six splendid newspapers, and the one great newspaper, which serve the world as models of responsible public information. I am speaking of the local press which in hundreds of American communities is the only printed news available.

Why do I think network TV does a better job of informing than these papers? Well, let's get the partisan bit over with. Television lives on advertising to an even greater extent than newspapers, and since advertising is big business, advertising is by nature Republican. Yet nowhere in network newscasts or network commentaries have I encountered the intense partisanship, the often-rabid bias that colors the editorial pages of the majority of newspapers in this country.

Now, very often, television coverage of news is superficial and inadequate. Very often the picture takes precedence over the point. But by and large, network news reports and commentaries make every effort to present viewers with more than one aspect of an issue, either by letting opposing spokesmen have their say, or by outlining the positions held by both major parties on the subject involved.

Television also provides a wide range of opinion by setting up four or five experts and letting them knock each other down. What has the local press of this nature? Is it discharging its duty to diversity by printing snippets of opinion from unqualified readers? Is this exploring an issue?

A newspaper has the duty to assume an attitude, to take a position, and also to go on to explain that position in light of an opposing one, bolstering it not with emotion but with fact.

Here, of course, is where background information helps the public to draw its conclusions. TV does a great deal of this in the form of documentaries, and you can say that they have the time and the money to do this and you haven't. Yet across this wide country, and with the exception of a handful of syndicated columns, I fail to find in any local paper any attempt, however minimal, to strengthen this muscle of digestion, without which news can neither nourish nor inform. It can only stuff. Between the opinions of the editor and the bare statements of the wire services there is nothing, nothing, that is, except a collection of snippets used as fillers between the ads and picked at random.

One of the greatest and most justified criticisms of television has been that in appealing to the largest audience possible, it neglects minority audiences and minority tastes. This remains true. And yet there are more programs that an intelligent man or woman can enjoy and derive interest from. In my trips, I pick up the local paper to find this enjoyment, in vain. Now, surely there's something wrong here. Many of these places are college communities where highly talented people live. What is there for them in the paper, usually the only paper, of their town? What features are provided for them? When a local paper has a monopoly in a region, as most of them do, why is it necessary to aim at the lowest common denominator?

I believe that newspapers have become a habit rather than a function. They have held their franchise so long that change has become inadmissible. I do not know, in fact, of any medium that has changed as little as the daily press. And this resistance to change is the end of growth, which, in turn, marks the end of usefulness.

Change means trouble, work, cost. It is easier to print wire-service dispatches than have a reporter on the beat. It is easier to buy syndicated columns than find and train local talent. It is easier to let the ads dictate the format than develop a format that elevates news above dog food. It is easier to write editorial copy that appeals to emotion rather than reason. And, in handling straight news, it is easier to assume the pious mantle of objectivity than to edit.

This is, to me, a tragedy. I am a printed-word woman myself, and I still think the word was not only in the beginning but will be in the end. No picture can ever be an adequate substitute. The word will prevail, if you, its guardians, treat it with the respect it deserves. For if you degrade and cheapen the word too long, people will turn to the picture. Oh, they will buy your papers, to hold up at breakfast or to line the trash can or to light a fire. But not to learn. And you may wake up one day to find that you have lost, to television, the power to inform a free people.

THE CONQUEST
OF TRIGGER MORTIS

The ruling, now historic, was passed in 1970, over the total opposition of the TV and radio networks and after ten years of controversy, six investigations, 483 juvenile murders, and the complete reorganization of the Federal Communications Commission. What finally pushed it through was the discovery of *trigger mortis* in a number of American children born in widely separated areas. In this malformation, the index finger is hooked permanently, forcing partial contraction of the whole hand in the position required for grasping a revolver. "The gun," said a distinguished anthropologist, "has become an extension of the American arm."

This mutation has been suspected some time before by others, who noted that as early as 1959, American toy manufacturers sold more than $60 million worth of guns and revolvers, and that on any day on television there were more than fifteen programs devoted to violence, and that in each of these programs, a gun was fired at least once and usually several times. The only difference between the programs was that in some the shooting was done out of doors and often from horses, and that in others it was done in hotel rooms, bars, or apartments. The first category was called "a Western" and was considered a wholesome fight between good men and bad men in a healthy country; the second was called Crime and Detective and was considered salubrious in its repeated implication that "crime does not pay."

Before the ruling on *trigger mortis,* television violence was believed by most experts to be of minimal importance as a contributory cause of youthful killing. Psychiatrists, social workers, program directors, advertisers, and sponsors had a handy set of arguments to prove their point. These (with translation appended) were the most popular:

Delinquency is a complex problem. No single factor is responsible. (Don't let's act. Let's not lose money.)

It's all a matter of the home. (Blame the parents. Blame the neighborhood. Blame poverty.)

Crime and adventure are a necessary outlet for natural childhood aggressions. (Keep the little bastards quiet while Mummy fixes supper.)

We don't really know what influences children. (Let's wait until they kill somebody.)

Only disturbed or abnormal children are affected by what they see on television. (And they are in a minority, so let their psychiatrists worry about them.)

Everybody was very pleased with these conclusions. For years, in spite of cries of alarm and protests from parents and a number of plain citizens, there were always enough experts to assure the public that crime and violence had nothing to do with crime and violence.

Dialogues like the following were frequent in congressional hearings:

SENATOR: In your opinion, what is the effect of these Westerns on children?

EXPERT: No one knows anything about it.

SENATOR: Well, you know that little children, six, seven, eight years old now have belts with guns. Do you think that this is due to them seeing these Westerns and all this shooting?

EXPERT: Oh, undoubtedly.

Psychiatrist Fredric Wertham, from whose book, *The Circle of Guilt,* the above was quoted, began a relentless campaign against what he called, in another book, *The Seduction of the Innocent.* In attacking the slogan "It's all up to the home," he wrote.

Of course the home has a lot to do with it. But is it wrong to accuse the home in the usual abstract way, for the home is inseparable from other social circumstances to which it is itself vulnerable. A hundred years ago the home could guard the children's safety; but with the new technological advances, the modern parent cannot possibly carry this responsibility. We have traffic regulations, school buses, school zones, and police to protect children from irresponsible drivers. Who will guard the child today from irresponsible adults who sell him incentives, blueprints, and weapons for delinquency?

But Wertham was dismissed by many of his colleagues and by much of the public as a man obsessed; too aggressively and intemperately committed to one cause, the rape of children's minds by mass communication, to be seriously considered. Thirty murders a day continued on home screens.

Next came, from the Nuffield Foundation in England, a thick book called *Television and the Child*, by Hilde T. Himmelweit, A. N. Oppenheim, and Pamela Vince. The authors did not confine themselves to programming specifically for children, since it had long been obvious in England, as it was here, that children usually watched adult programs in preference to "kiddie shows." In more than four hundred pages of meticulous research, they came to certain conclusions, which were the basis for further evidence that led, ten years later, to government intervention into broadcasting practices. Here are a few of their findings about the 20 percent of programs seen by children in their peak viewing hours that are devoted to aggression and violence:

At the center of preoccupation with violence is the gun, which spells power, makes people listen, and forces them to do what is wanted.

It is said that these programmes have two main desirable effects: they teach the lesson that crime does not pay, and they provide a harmless outlet through fantasy for the child's hostile feelings. We take issue with both statements. The lesson as taught in these programmes is entirely negative (it is best not to offend the law). To present such a one-sided view, repeated week after week, is contrary to the recognized educational principle that a moral lesson, to be effective, must teach what should be done as well as what should not be done.

More serious is the fact that the child may learn... that to shoot, bully, and cheat is allowed, provided one is on the right side of the law, and that relationships among people are built not on loyalty but on fear and domination.

As for being a "harmless outlet for aggressive feelings," the authors, quoting the testimony of Dr. Eleanor E. Maccoby of Harvard that this discharge in fantasy alters nothing in the child's real life, write that when aggressive feelings exist, "they are not as a rule discharged on viewing crime and violence."

The Nuffield Report authors had obviously fallen into the error of blaming the industry instead of the child. "Beefs," "squawks," the broadcasters called these surges of protest year after year. But their biggest defense became, in the end, their undoing. They had assured themselves that by removing the physical effects of violence, it was stripped of harm. They showed no blood, no close-ups of open wounds, no last convulsions of a riddled body. Men were shot, they clapped their hands to their stomachs, and either fell forwards or backwards as the camera panned away and returned to the gun. And while the broadcasters felt this a noble concession to the sensibilities of young viewers ("Brutality or physical agony," says the NBC Code, "is not presented in detail nor indicated by offensive sound or visual effects"), they were in actuality presenting, day after day, two great immoralities: that shooting is clean, and easy. To pull a trigger requires neither strength, skill, nor courage: it is the bullet that kills. And to kill with a gun is quick and painless. Hero or criminal, both were cowards who answered questions by pulling triggers. This was the daily lesson for sixty million children for twenty years.

Until, of course, the people finally rose. Some cool legal heads first managed to draft legislation banning the sale of pornographic and sensational printed material without curbing individual liberty or preventing the sale of *Lady Chatterley's Lover* or Aristophanes. Then came the famous FCC ruling, Bylaw A 41-632. In effect, this gave the FCC the power to revoke the license of any broadcaster showing fictionalized killing without also displaying the natural consequences to the person killed. Showing gore meant that the sponsor would not sell many goods. It was therefore far easier to cut out guns entirely.

Far easier, that is, for everyone but the writers. After the law was put into effect, there was mass unemployment among television writers in Hollywood and New York. They had relied so long on their collaborator, the gun, that they were incapable of writing a plot without it. Suddenly, the poor writers had to think up situations where people and ideas provided excitement instead of a Colt 45. It was a period of anguish none of them will forget.

Disarmament, at least of the young, was finally a fact. Briefly. Now the worst of old Westerns are recycling as space epics in which only robots die, and children watch animated comic strips in which blasters spew out death rays against... yep, bad men. And the advent of the video cassette recorder means that any movie, however violent, may be rented for home viewing six months after its initial release in theaters.

LOOPHOLE

*Two psychiatrists were denied tax
deductions for getting psychonalyzed. . . .
Under the tax law, education expenses are
deductible when intended to improve one's
skills in an existing job, but not to prepare
for a better one.*

Can a painter who is painted claim deductions?
Can seducers who'er seduced deduct seductions?
Can a writer, written of, write off this writing
As a necessary lesson in backbiting?

Can a preacher who is preached at claim exemption
For thus furthering his practice of redemption?

How infinitely logical, what fun to
Deduct in kind for what one has been done to!

BORN FREAK

If you don't know who Ookie is, you don't read animal news, and if you don't read animal news you don't know how superior it is to human news. You also don't belong to a quite sizable group of citizens who have such an affinity with other species that they concern themselves deeply with the trials and fortunes of cats, dogs, lions, apes, birds, and fish.

For me, this all started with early exposure to Wagner. A solemn tot, I was greatly impressed with the fact that Siegfried could understand the speech of birds after drinking Fafner's blood. The means distressed me but the end seemed wholly desirable (although in later years I have come to doubt the stimulation of bird talk). And I have been plagued ever since with the feeling that I could communicate directly with animals not by potions but by empathy. I have succeeded to the extent of feeling on many occasions that my ears were lying back, my tail twitching, my fur rising, and my lips drawn back from my teeth. I have also succeeded in imagining myself in a pool with Ookie.

Ookie is a baby walrus at the Coney Island Aquarium who looks like Teddy Roosevelt and can do more things with an empty beer cask than Teddy could. Ookie is deeply interested in life and very fond of attention, and perhaps the only thing we don't share is whiskers and a diet of mashed haddock and cod-liver oil. But I am touched by Ookie's faith in man and furious at the little ruffians who throw balls in the pool that might choke her. I can feel that ball in my throat as I gasp for air.

I have also been very concerned with the female whale who was caught off Coney and put in the pool and who swam counterclockwise with her eyes closed from then on. Sick whales grieve me: there is such a volume of woe.

And speaking of volume, I identified strongly with an elephant during the recent bomb-alarm practice in New York. There was a photograph of a keeper pushing him into shelter, and I never saw a more resistant backside in my life. My friend, I thought; my brother.

I am, in fact, always with the animals: with the bull against the matador, the monkey who escapes, the dog who bites the visitor, the hippo who sulks, and the platypus who will not lay. In my identification with nearly all creatures I don't know that I could go as far as Dr. Lorenz and mother geese, but I can easily imagine an eccentric senescence surrounded by a large variety of animals whose thoughts I can come to understand and whose love I will elicit. The closing years will be absorbing, if messy.

But till now, my major obsession has been big cats: I have always wanted to rear a lion. Never mind why; analysis could shadow an otherwise sunny subject. Anyway, the nearest I've come to this dream was to hold a six-month-old male cub on my lap in the Berlin Zoo and scratch his chin. His name was Max, he purred like a generator, and peace entered my heart at last. But Max grew heavy on my knees and the zoo closed and so did this moment of triumph.

It remained for a Mrs. Adamson to do what I had failed to do and write a book about it called *Born Free* (Pantheon, $4.95). It is about Elsa, a lioness whom she and her husband, the senior game warden in the Northern Frontier Province of Kenya, reared from a blind and motherless cub to maturity and freedom.

Elsa is a great girl and Joy Adamson is a remarkable woman, and I read of their relationship with sustained and breathless attention. I was right to love lions: they are beautiful and majestic and intelligent and they have a sense of humor and the capacity to love. At least Elsa did. But after *Born Free*, I have reluctantly laid to rest my ambition to establish close relations with a lion. There appear to be more than the usual obstacles to rearing a large carnivore in a small apartment, not the least of them a husband who is not a game warden and does not warm to cats. Mr. Adamson shot the animals for Elsa's snacks, and although my husband is very handy with a rifle, I doubt whether there is anything in Central Park or the eastern end of Long Island that would keep Agnes nourished for long. (Agnes is the lion I might have had.) Like the Adamsons, we would not want to encourage in Agnes a taste for people, plentiful and expendable as they are.

There are several traits in Elsa that I found disturbing, too. One was a habit of sucking Mrs. Adamson's thumb when she was nervous; that is, when Elsa was nervous. Holding a thumb still for long periods is time-consuming, and I'm simply too busy. Then, Elsa grew accustomed to sharing Mrs. Adamson's bed at night and for naps, and there are wonderful pictures of her resting her large tufted chin on her friend's neck and draping a monumental paw over her waist. I can understand the feeling of security this might give, but what about a husband? Indeed, Elsa occasionally spent the night in *Mr.* Adamson's bed, but the basic problem remains: one is not alone.

Then there was the business of Elsa's humor. She was full of loving pranks, one of them being to hurl herself against people at full speed and send them sprawling. She also practiced a jujitsu trick on guests by felling them with one neat swipe of the paw on their ankle. These sallies are greeted with hearty laughter by the Adamsons, but I feel my circle of friends would diminish sharply if Agnes did that. They are out of training.

ISN'T
ANYTHING
OBSCENE
ANYMORE?

It was very sad about Mlle. Fleuri. As a member of the Charm Corps sent by the Common Market Countries to raise the standard of living in the United States, she had the poor judgment to jot down notes on the back of a Four Seasons' menu, which was found subsequently by a busboy and distributed widely.

"I am very glad to be among these friendly people," she wrote, "but I was never prepared for the kind of vulgarity you find here in the streets and homes. It is truly distressing to see girls of good families chewing gum and rich suburban ladies appearing in public with their hair on rollers. And the language of the children! There appears to be no refinement of behavior here commensurate with the possession of money and comforts."

An outraged public demanded Mlle. Fleuri's immediate ouster, and she went back to Neuchatel in tears. Americans found particularly intolerant the two words "vulgarity" and "refinement." If Mlle. Fleuri had been better briefed, she would have known that both words implied standards of judgment incompatible with a democratic society since they reek of distinction, of class above class.

Vulgarity, which I suppose is one caste step above obscenity, although both have become synonymous, remains a valid adjective, and I commend Mlle. Fleuri's use of it to describe the many forms of boorishness and coarseness which are accepted precisely because they are common, another adjective that, in juxtaposition to people, has become offensive.

It is just as well that Mlle. Fleuri did not remain a few seasons to experience our contemporary theater. At a first night in New York,

194

the actors in a new play take off their clothes and scream obscenities at the audience, while a critic removes *his* clothes and sits naked in his seat.

In another play, a naked man and woman approximate the sex act, and in another, two men engage in erotic intimacies.

One of the biggest best sellers of recent history concerns a man whose single obsessive passion, masturbation, makes him incapable of love.

In a majority of new films, naked sex scenes, heterosexual, incestuous, or homosexual, are staples, and in many of them, as in the theatre, elements of sadomasochism are present.

As for the medium of print, anyone, child or adult, can buy at any big city newsstand not only the slick publications offering male and female bodies in lavish display, but a growing number of underground papers filled with four-letter words and explicit pictures. In any bookstore in the less fashionable sections of a city, paperbacks catering to all conceivable erotic or sadistic tastes are available.

We have, in short, now reached a state in our society where anything goes, where all is permitted, and where no limits are placed on the appetites of the individual, on the gratification of his desires and fantasies. Girls chewing gum and suburban mavens shopping with rollers in their hair are the least of it. The old notion of refinement, a kind of carriage, a way of moving and dressing, a use of voice and hands, that proclaimed a being superior in perception and attainment, is lamentably archaic.

Disgusting? Dangerous? There ought to be a law? A lot of Americans are saying this, while others are applauding the current wide-open market as the inevitable and rightful extension of personal freedom. The argument for the unrestricted dissemination of pornography and obscenity, held by many of the most thoughtful citizens of this democratic society, is a cogent one.

"Obscenity for whom?" they say. A word shocking to a church-going housewife in Kansas is normal speech for a Texas oilman.

Although words describing sexual functions are largely used in curses, jokes, or in contempt, they are dirty only to those for whom sex is dirty.

At a time when our customs and codes of morality, whether sustained or imposed by church or family or school, have eroded, when the melting pot, once our proudest boast, the American miracle of many bloods becoming one, has become a witches' caldron of division and dissension, what were once called "community standards" no longer serve as moral guidelines applicable to all and enforceable by law.

That is why the highest courts and the most respected juridical minds have been unable to make definitions of "obscenity" and "pornography" precise enough for legislation. There can be no law discriminating against the hard-core pornography sweeping the country at immense profits to its purveyors that does not, at the same time, abrogate the freedom of the serious writer or artist to convey life as he sees it, and the right of the citizen to read it or see it.

But then, you say, what about children? Could there not at least be laws prohibiting the sale of such material to the young?

How young? And how to prohibit? Anyone who has listened to the talk of today's schoolchildren must know their familiarity with obscenity and their sexual awareness. No home, however nice, can screen them from this pollution or curb this precocity. So the law is no answer—or rather, a very dangerous one in terms of our constitution.

To discriminate between healthy freedom and sick license has become an act of courage at this particular time. Anybody who now admits to being shocked or repelled by any facet of pornography or obscenity is by automatic definition a square, a throwback, a blue-nose, a puritan. The road to sensual awareness, it seems, is to bludgeon sensibility and obliterate taste.

Yet that very sensibility is what makes a civilized human being. It is a sad comment on a university education and the climate of this illiterate age that both old and young must resort to obscenity instead of discourse to communicate.

Isn't there a line, not determined by law but by each individual's deepest instinct, to be drawn somewhere? And if so, how? What are the determinants?

Nudity per se is not at issue here. Nor the sex act, however practiced. Nor four-letter words. The determinant is not what is done, or said, or shown, but for what reason and in what context. What is obscene is not two naked people making love on screen or onstage; it is the sexual act used as a come-on, without in any way enlarging our knowledge of the characters involved or the nature of love.

The real obscenity, to my mind, occurs when, in act or speech, sex itself (and, most usually, woman) becomes the object of contempt, when sadism enters in, when aggression is committed against the human body or human spirit. Sadistic pornography is an act of violence *against* sex. It is the violation and abuse of the body of a man or woman, foreign to the act of love. Obscenity for its own sake, or the sake of shock, if that is still possible, is an act of violence against language. Both are perversions and diminutions of the human spirit. Both are ugly.

What concerns me is the virulence with which any talk of restraint is equated immediately with censorship, with which any reservations as to freedom of expression are damned as nice-nelly-isms, the last gasp of the puritan ethos, or the first heralds of a police state.

Take the case of the writer Pamela Hansford Johnson (the wife of Sir Charles Snow), who reported on the Moors Trial in England. This concerned a Manchester couple who were ultimately convicted of the torture, sexual abuse, and murder of three young children, whom they then buried on the moors. The couple were ardent disciples of work of the Marquis de Sade, and owners of a rich store of pornography of a predominantly sadomasochistic nature.

So shaken and sickened was Pamela Hansford Johnson by the trial of this couple that she wrote a small book, *On Iniquity,* in which she raised the question as to whether total public access to writing of this nature might not ultimately destroy the last inhibitory factors that make a civilized society, and whether the perpetrators would have committed these terrible and senseless murders if they had not had free access to the printed sanction of torture, perversion, and killing.

Although she at no time counseled censorship, she did suggest the need of self-restraint on the part of publishers of such material, and of the distribution process by which it could be acquired with the greatest of ease by the growing legion of mentally and emotionally disturbed in our midst.

Well, the lady and her little book were torn apart. She was upperclass, she was muddled, she was emotional, she was unrealistic, and so forth. However, she did have a few defenders. Although he took exception to some of her reasoning, a critic in the *Manchester Guardian* said this: "I see no way to rebut her main propositions. The imagination cannot be made a private preserve of the arts and entertainment industry, exempt from moral scrutiny; because moral consequences, of the most crudely moral kind, do follow from imaginative acts. In the Moors murder case, the evidence compels us to make a connection between what the couple read and what they did."

Miss Hansford Johnson's book was an attack on a certain group of intellectuals who have substituted the idea of sickness for the idea of sin, because they disregard the social consequences of the individual's inner choices. They attribute glamour to violence, to madness, to evil, to every form of dissent from conventional pieties.

It is such people, and we have them here in abundance, who bear responsibility for the spiritual chaos in which we are now living; a climate in which we are responsible for nothing beyond our own enlargement of experience. (Doing your own thing.)

It is revealing that the public for "soft pornography" is not so much the young as those older Americans who are the first to decry the rising tide of obscenity. Now free to read openly what so many have dreamed of furtively, they are a sad commentary on the taboos and the hypocrises that molded them. It is they, rather than the young, who have made the spread of pornography a multimillion-dollar industry.

In fact, it is quite possible that in the light of sex education and the open expression of sexual drives among young people, this market in filth, "soft" and "hard," will wither away. Since the kids know everything and since nothing is forbidden, who needs it? They can take sex in their stride, And when they can throw away the crutch of obscenity as a substitute for speech, even the four-letter press may wither, too.

In the meantime, let's call a spade a spade. There *is* pornography, there *is* obscenity, and neither has anything to do with the honest sexuality and the freedom of expression that are essential to full human and social development.

Which brings me back to Mlle. Fleuri. In the unlikely event that she returned to us on another crusade, she might despair to write even on a menu, taking the first Concorde home. And who could blame her?

THE COMPACT CAR

"Ford, General Motors and Chrysler are reported prepared to spend 10 million dollars each on introducing their Falcon, Corvair and Valiant." —
Printers Ink

It's mighty expensive, it seems, to make clear
Which engine's in front and which sits in the rear.
An arrow says Ford that is weighted in front
Flies straight, while a back-weighted arrow just won't,
Implying that the Falcon is safer by far
Than the rear-powered Corvair, the Chevrolet car;
And Chrysler is pointing with scorn at the tail
Of the Volkswagen, Renault, and Fiat, which fail
(According to Chrysler) to properly steer,
Since their engines, alas, are encased in the rear;
While General Motors, in counterattack,
Claims a quieter ride with the boost in the back.
Whatever the outcome, the roads will be full
Of nice little engines that push cars or pull,
And no one need squander ten million to find
The relative merits of front or behind.

HOW WELL DO
ADVERTISERS
KNOW
THE CONSUMING
PUBLIC?
(A SPEECH)
October 15, 1963

Most speakers start off with a joke, but until now I've never been able to think of one. This time I have.

The joke is that I'm here. In case you haven't heard, the advertising profession views me as a sort of creeping plague— something that gets under their shirts and itches. Why, even such eminent figures as Woodrow Wirsig and Walter Weir have singled me out in their public writings as a mush-headed dreamer, out of touch with today's realities and—worst of all—unaware that advertising is the single greatest contribution to human welfare.

This is unjust. I know what advertising has done. It has made us smell good, look good, and live good—like a citizen should. Advertising does great because the agencies are. See? I'm no mush-head. What's more, advertising does not—contrary to some detractors—concern itself only with material values. I understand that in the Middle West the Presbyterian Church is running a test campaign to find out whether advertising can interest more people in religion. Apparently Stan Freberg is writing the jingles, one of which contains the uplifting line: "Doesn't it get a little lonely sometimes— out on that limb without Him?"

Inspired by this I've made up a few jingles myself. Try Prayer— it purifies the air. Take Belief—for fast, fast, *fast* Relief.

Or what about this: Left in the lurch? No help from Birch? Try

Church. And now, the weather...

I shall now—with some difficulty—be serious. The question I'm supposed to kick around today is How Well Do Advertisers Know the Consuming Public? Considering the volume of sales that makes this country the most prosperous in the world, the answer should be obvious: They know us very well. Heaven knows, the American consumer has for years been the object of an unrelenting scrutiny that measures everything from his salary to his saliva, from his pulse to his surprise, from his libido to his liver. Now they've got a secret eye-camera that checks up on your pupil dilations. A fellow looks at a package of Fig Newtons, say, and if he likes Fig Newtons, his pupils dilate, and if he doesn't they contract. The marketing people say this little camera is much more reliable than the consumer, who—presumably—is a natural-born liar. They mention the case of a man who said he preferred a business magazine article to a racier item in a man's magazine, but when he was shown the racier item—I wonder what that could have been?—his eyes dilated. I guess this proved that he liked nudes better than news. It's marvelous what science is doing.

Anyway, with or without these Peeping Tom techniques, advertisers do know a lot of basic things about us people. They know that women like to be thin but would rather eat cream-fudge layer cake. They know that men want to look virile but would rather be comfortable. They know that people want dry beer instead of wet beer. They know that children want everything—and get it.

But there are an amazing amount of things they don't know. Things they don't need to be told by secret cameras or personality tests, by poll or survey. Things that ordinary observation of daily life should tell them. Things that an elementary understanding of human nature should make clear.

I'd like to start with some examples, and if they apply to television rather than to print, it is partly because advertising on TV reaches the greatest number of consumers and has therefore the widest overall impact; and partly because I think that television

advertising lags considerably behind printed advertising in its assess-
ment of—and appeal to—the consumer.

Take this hair-tint commercial, for instance. There's this row of
suburban homes, see, and you see two wives waiting in their
neighboring doorways to greet two commuting husbands back from
a tough day in the city and three bar-car martinis.

Well, we close in on one of the wives, and she's a very pretty
woman indeed with an interesting streak in her hair and a sweet
smile on her face. The husband of the other woman walks by with a
bunch of flowers for *his* mate, but *her* husband is empty-handed. Her
smile vanishes as she thinks out loud: Is it my gray streak? Her tragic
face fades out. We see her next having washed her gray away and
become a varnished brunette dressed to the teeth and arranging
roses in a vase. Enter husband in dinner jacket and leer. Wife sticks
one rose in husband's lapel, husband takes it out and sticks it in his
teeth. They do a revolting little dance together, he wraps her in
mink, and they waltz off to a night on the town. Now everything in
this little concoction is the sheerest nonsense, and every viewer
knows it. Men do not neglect their wives because they have a gray
streak. (There are fifty better reasons.) Men do not stick roses in
their teeth after a hard day at the office. Men very rarely bring
flowers back on the 6:10 anyway, even to blondes. But there's
something much worse than that here: a distortion of values that will
make women worry about the wrong things in life. There are a
hundred ways of selling hair tint without making love depend on it.
And advertisers, in general, bear a large part of the responsibility for
the deep feelings of inadequacy that drive women to psychiatrists,
pills, or the bottle. You keep telling us over and over that if only we
would use that or have this or look like that, we would be forever
desirable, forever happy. So we spend our times worrying over the
gray streak or the extra pound or the dry skin instead of our minds,
our hearts, and our fellow men.

Now back to the little screen for further evidence of advertiser
ignorance of the consumer. They don't know children. Children do

not come rushing home to their parents shouting "Mom, our group had twenty percent less cavities than the others!" Little boys do not know the difference between scratchy towels and soft towels because they seldom use them. Big boys don't either. In fact, big boys—or men—do not notice when their shirts are whiter. They don't notice laundry at all unless their buttons are torn off. The whole subject of wash and detergents is a big yawning bore to the male, and any female dumb enough to bring her new bleaches into the conversation will not latch onto him long.

But the real area of stupefying advertiser ignorance of the consumer is the biggest one of all: women. They are, of course, the prime targets, because they are the prime buyers. And gentlemen, if I may call you that, you don't know us at all.

For one thing, out of the nearly forty-three million wives in this country, over fourteen million of us work. But you, the advertisers, continue to assume that all American women are housewives only, bound in perpetuity to sink, stove, and nursery. I have yet to see an ad or commercial in which the woman involved buys a product because it helps her speed up her chores after a working day. I have yet to see any reference or any mention of the fact that these fourteen million women who have jobs need certain products even more than her home-bound and time-free sister. There is in advertising no recognition of this major social and economic fact: that more and more women have jobs as well as homes and that they constitute a large, enlightened and demanding consumer group which should be recognized as, and appealed to, as such.

For another thing, over one hundred forty thousand women are college alumnae and many millions are high school graduates— and presumably educated. But I have yet to see a commercial in which a woman lays down a book or leaves a piano or interrupts her needlepoint in order to get on with some household chore. Nor, for that matter, have I seen any woman in a commercial with an IQ over 95. According to advertisers, women are a garrulous, scatterbrained bunch of suckers who have nothing to do but polish and cook, and nothing to talk about but soap and food.

Is this a true image of the American woman? And if it isn't, are you deliberately trying to make it so in order to sell more products? If you are, you are doing not only us but the nation a disservice. For I don't think the advertisers have any real idea of their power not only to reflect, but to mold, society. And if you reflect us incorrectly, as I believe you are doing, you are raising a generation of children with cockeyed values as to what men and women and life and family really are. You may be training them as consumers but you are certainly not educating them as people.

And don't say that your job is to sell and not educate. I have the word of Hugh Downs himself, in a speech to the Alberto-Culver sales meeting in Chicago recently, in which he says that "the promotion of a good product is a form of education and a form that serves truth in the same way as promotion of an ethical ideal."

Are you serving truth, for instance, when not one of the nineteen million blacks in this country is shown on television as a consumer of products? Can't colored housewives have laundry, wash diapers, wax floors, bake layer-cakes? Don't colored girls want to look beautiful? Don't blacks buy beer? Is there any good reason why men might not vote for a lovely dark Miss Rheingold?

But still, in all your advertising, you—or I really should say the sponsors—persist in showing a white middle-class suburban world of two-car garages, white-collar husbands, and aproned women, when the real, turbulent, fascinating, pluralistic world that is America tells a vastly different story.

And what about that very hot potato, cigarette advertising? Some of you—for obvious reasons and millions of dollars—still refuse to admit that the link between smoking and cancer—which the highest scientific bodies in several countries have officially established—does indeed exist. You go right on television, at hours when children are looking, showing young, handsome people puffing away as if smoking was the normal, healthy romantic way of life. It goes with status and love and youth and pretty country and all pleasant things. So naturally, the minute a kid is fourteen he wants to smoke, too.

Now, I have noticed that one advertiser is trying to make his male smokers—on TV and in print—the mature types (what is the slogan—separating the men from the boys?)—in the naïve belief that only adults will be encouraged to indulge. But don't all boys want to ape grown men—in clothes, in cars, in talk—and certainly in habits? Do you really think that this kind of pitch is going to escape them?

Now, everybody knows that millions of adults like to smoke and have no intention of stopping for any reason. Certainly, cigarette manufacturers have every intention of continuing to cater to this popular human indulgence, whatever its hazards. But the hazards are real, the danger is there, and it would seem to me that the advertiser who cares about his consumer would devise some means of letting him know this.

I am not naïve enough—contrary to my detractors—to think that cigarette advertising will—or should—cease. But I am interested enough in the fate of my fellow Americans to suggest that advertisers seriously consider new approaches to selling this highly controversial product. In England, for instance, cigarette advertising on TV is confined to late evening hours when children are presumably not viewing. but there are other approaches, too. Would not this kind of slogan get the right message across: A Habit is Not a Pleasure: Don't Smoke Because You *Have* To: Smoke because You *Want* To? Surely the theme of moderation is the answer: Don't Be Hooked—Be Healthy. Smoke Less and Enjoy It More....Maybe I am just a frustrated copywriter. Anyway, my charge for this deathless copy runs into six figures.

But again, seriously, my quarrel with advertisers is really this: that they do not realize the power they have. And I don't mean the power to move goods. I don't even mean the power, which they have exercised to their credit and the nation's economy—to raise the standard of living in this country beyond anything man has yet seen.

The power I mean is the power to affect — deeply and lastingly — the nature, attitudes, and aspirations of a hundred and eighty million Americans. For years advertisers have been conditioning us not just to buy certain things but to live and think and aspire in certain ways.

On the material level, these ways have been largely good. On the human or spiritual or moral level, I am not at all sure they are. And I do not mean here the problem of misleading or deceptive advertising: on the whole, most products perform as they are claimed to do; for if they didn't people would stop buying them. No, I am referring to a misleading and deceptive view of life and people that could, in the long run, be detrimental to American society. For it is not enough to show people how to *live* better: there is a mandate for any group with enormous powers of communication to show people how to *be* better. The two are not incompatible, but they can be divorced and they are being divorced by the foolish images of American home life that we see day in and day out on the TV screen or the pages of magazines.

And in this connection, I would like to point out what one form of advertising is doing to the nation's children and their relationships to their parents. In the last years (and I am quoting a *New York Times* article) researchers have found that 94 percent of mothers interviewed said their children demanded that they buy certain items they had seen advertised on television. Great, you say, what a market: forty million children becoming consumers from the age of three onward!

But it's not great. It's creating a race of demanding, nagging, overindulged, overpampered kids — and a race of beaten-down, spineless parents who take their orders. Even the advertisers are beginning to see this. One man, Mr. Charles Goldschmidt, the chairman of an agency, said "I think some advertisers are trying too hard to appease the kids."

How right he is. And what a major disservice this kind of appeasement is to any decent sense of values. You, the advertisers, have a mandate to teach values of more than your product. Infinitely more people get your messages than read the editorial contents of magazines or look—and I mean really look—at most television programs. They may think they watch the programs, but what stays with them are the unending interruptions: the commercial kiddies who whine for fried chicken when their mother has cooked them something else; the half-witted housewife who doesn't know she's on camera; the irritable man who has acid indigestion; the miserable man who can't breathe; the saccharine mothers and daughters who look alike (but I bet don't think alike); the overdressed young lovers who smoke by waterfalls;...you name it, we get it. And it's a wholesale perversion of reality.

Oh—sometimes it isn't. Whoever thought up the small boy who prefers Oreos to little girls was on the right track. And so was the fellow who showed little kids viewing the new baby in the family with considerable distaste. Some of your advertisers—and many in the print media—have kept your eyes and ears open and sold your product in a real world to real people. You are the ones with respect for your fellow Americans as well as for your product. And you are to be saluted.

So, I may say, are your sponsors...who, in the last analysis, are the ones we've been talking about all the time. I suspect that the sponsor, and not the advertiser, is the real culprit in the manufacture of this advertising dreamworld.

Believe it or not, until today some of my best friends were advertisers. They are a lively, observant, sophisticated lot who, left to themselves, would probably not produce the nonsense they do. But let's face it: they need the accounts more than they need my approval—or even the gratitude of millions of consumers who have suffered the tedious stereotypes and endless repetitions of so many of their commercials.

So, you see, I am really very pro-advertisers. All I want is that they cast the scales off their eyes, see the world as it is—and sell honesty to the sponsor as the best way not only to move his product but to benefit the health, education and welfare of an entire nation.

They have the power—and the obligation—to do so.

But they can't do it until they take a new, long, hard, fresh look at us—the consumers—so that we can recognize ourselves as we really are.

THE THIN
GRAY LINE

"Aw, they all do it," growled the cabdriver. He was talking about cops who took payoffs for winking at double parking, but his cynicism could as well have been directed at any of a dozen other instances of corruption, big-time and small-time. Moreover, the disgust in his voice was overlaid by an unspoken "So what?": the implication that since this was the way things were, there was nothing anybody could do.

Like millions of his fellow Americans, the cabdriver was probably a decent human being who had never stolen anything, broken any law, or willfully injured another; somewhere, a knowledge of what was probably right had kept him from committing what was clearly wrong. But that knowledge had not kept a thin gray line that separates the two conditions from becoming daily grayer and thinner, to the point almost of imperceptibility.

The same citizen who voices his outrage at police corruption will slip the traffic cop on his block a handsome Christmas present in the belief (so far sustained) that his car, nestled under a "No Parking" sign, will not be ticketed. The son of that nice woman next door has a habit of stealing cash from her purse because his allowance is smaller than his buddies'. Your own son's best friend admitted cheating at exams because "most of them do."

Bit by bit, the resistance to and immunity against wrong that a healthy social body builds up by law and ethics and the dictation of conscience have broken down. And instead of the fighting indignation of a people outraged by those who prey on them, we have the admission of impotence: "They all do it."

How did we get this way? What started this blurring of what was once a thick black line between the lawful and the lawless? What makes "a regular guy" accept a bribe? What makes a nice kid take money for something he knows is not only illegal but wrong, like throwing a basketball game?

When you look into the background of an erring "kid," you will often find a comfortable home and a mother who will tell you, with tears in her eyes, that she "gave him everything." She probably did, to his eternal damage. She began the process of corruption by bribing his love with things, money, the granting of his wishes. Fearing her son's disapproval, the indulgent mother denies him nothing except responsibility. Instead of growing up, he grows to believe that the world owes him everything.

The nice kid's father crosses the thin gray line himself in a dozen ways, day in and day out. He pads his expenses on his income-tax returns as a matter of course. As a landlord, he pays the local inspectors of the city housing authority to overlook violations on the properties he rents. When his son flunks his driving test, he gives him ten dollars to slip to the inspector on his second test. "They all do it," he says.

The nice kid is brought up with boys and girls who have no heroes except people not much older than themselves who have made the Big Time, usually in show business or sports. Publicity and money are the halos of their stars, who range from pop singers who can't sing to drugged ballplayers who can't read; from teen-age starlets who can't act to television performers who can't think. They may be excited by the exploits of spacemen, but the work's too tough and dangerous.

The nice kids have no heroes because they don't believe in heroes. Heroes are suckers and squares. To be a hero, you have to excel, to take risks, and, above all, not only choose between right and wrong, but defend the right and fight the wrong. This means responsibility, and who wants that?

Today, no one has to take any responsibility. The psychiatrists, the sociologists, the novelists, the playwrights have seen to that. Nobody is really to blame for what he does. It's society. It's environment. It's a broken home. It's an underprivileged area. But it's hardly ever you.

A fellow commits a crime because he's basically insecure, because he hated his stepmother at nine, or because his sister needs an operation. A policeman loots a store because his salary is too low. A city official accepts a payoff because it's offered to him. Members of minority groups, racial or otherwise, commit crimes because they are economically deprived or socially estranged.

The words "right" and "wrong" are foreign to this language. So is the definition of ethics as "man's normal state." So is conscience as "an inward monitor." In today's lexicon of behavior, conscience has an archaic a sound as the proverb, "Honesty is the best policy."

This is a matter that concerns the health and future of a nation. It involves the two-dollar illegal bettor as well as the corporation price-fixer, the college-examination cheater and the payroll-padding congressman, the expense-account chiseler and the undercover lobbyist, the seller of pornography and his schoolboy buyer, the compromised judge and the stealing delinquent. They may be a minority. But when the majority exempt themselves from responsibility by accepting corruption as natural ("They all do it"), this society is bordering on chaos. If the line between right and wrong is finally erased, there is no defense against the anarchy of evil.

Before this happens, and it is by no means far away, it might be well for the schools of the nation to substitute for the controversial prayer a daily lesson in ethics, law, and responsibility to society that would fortify conscience as exercise strengthens muscles. And it would be even better if parents were compelled to attend. For corruption is not something you read about in the papers and leave to the courts. We are all involved.

ANIMAL
BEHAVIORISM

"An experiment of the Korinth Agricultural School has shown that if pigs get eight shots a day of Danish potato whisky they 'acquire an optimistic view of life.' A teacher at the school said the pigs develop a strong liking for alcohol and get very cheerful"— New York Herald Tribune ·

It only takes a swig
To sublimate a pig.
An alcoholic swill
Is now his greatest thrill,
An intermittent swallow
Far better than a wallow,
A tighter-curling tail
His signal of wassail,
The optimistic view
Engendered by it too.
To keep him in the pink
There's nothing like a dram.
Oh happy, happy swine,
Our brothers in decline!

THE DECLINE
OF STYLE

Dismiss "fashionable," which is ephemeral and external. Discard "stylish," the word itself a turn-of-the-century evocation of ladies with very small waists, very large hats, and very narrow minds. These have nothing to do with style, which I see as a way of speaking, walking, behaving, creating, and *being*, which is both highly personal and yet, through its commanding presence, able to color the social and cultural climate of others.

It has to do with "life-style," the climate of a new generation, only in that a few in the vast multitude of young conformists managed to emerge with that special signature which is part of style. In doing so they were timeless, conjuring visions of Regency dandies, medieval princes, Renaissance rakes. (Forget the fake Navahos, the handicraft shawls, and the poverty patches.

All right, who had style? Fred Astaire, Franklin D. Roosevelt, Emily Dickinson, Aldous Huxley, Richard Brinsley Sheridan, François Villon, a wildly disparate few in history's many. In trying to find out what they had in common, I would include form, clarity, grace, and that clear consciousness of self without which none can affect the quality of life.

Finally, people with style have managed to distill the essence of their gifts by imposing on themselves certain disciplines that refine rather than smother their instincts. They show us, as well, what is largely missed today. The common language of school or street is an inchoate mess of "like I said" and "y' know" and "like, man," interspersed with obscenities and other substitutes for thought.

Blame this on several things: a steep decline in reading as a result of laziness, the substitution of television, film and visual distractions (video game boards, light shows) for language, and the assumption that brotherhood consists of aping the ignorant.

At the other end, the jargons of sociology, psychiatry and other inexact sciences (including business) are arid, tedious, and without savor. The language of government and its leaders is a waste of platitudes and declarations, so void of pace, inflection, vitality, and form that the listening mind drifts before closing. Even our pornography lacks style.

A French philosopher, Joseph de Maistre, observed that "every individual or national degeneration is immediately revealed by a directly proportional degradation in language."

Here are some findings from tests made to determine how well Johnny can write:

Nine-year-old Americans show almost no command of the basic writing mechanics of grammar, vocabulary, spelling, sentence structure, and punctuation.

Even the best of seventeen-year-olds seldom display any flair or facility by moving beyond commonplace language.

One survey of 86,000 students found only four or five people with a really good command of the English language. Even these, who can write adequate business letters and personal notes, were judged as lacking "imagination, vitality, and detail."

As for public prose, particularly in fiction, coherence, clarity, and rhythmic line (in all but a few acknowledged masterpieces of these) are as contemputuously dismissed or ignored as the phrase "well-made" applied to a play.

On the contrary, most lavishly praised today is the non-style: an electric circus of schizoid images and fragmented sequence that is supposed to indicate powerful talent. The starts and stutters and wild inversions of a spastic mind are highly praised by critics bored by simplicity and easy reading.

As for legitimate boredom, what about architecture? Look at your cities: what style exists except for the few new skyscrapers with swoop and elegance or the few residential streets where houses survive from an era of dignity and proportion? And the rest? Vast cubes of commerce, purely functional, great blocks of apartments with filing cabinets for living and "balconies" for breathing carbon monoxide.

And what about people themselves? How have we managed at last to achieve a graceless society?

Partly because a new generation, rejecting deception, came to think of manners as a form of hypocrisy. Why ask "How are you?" when you don't give a damn? Why give up your bus seat to an old bag who can stand? "Please," "thank you," "excuse me,"—who's kiddin', man?

In more and more adults, whatever manners they once possessed have been eroded by the sheer pressures of daily living, crowds, noise, brutality on a massive scale in life, on screen, in print . . . all these and the daily hassle of job and transport have murdered those small amenities, the social lubricant.

Style is one thing more: bearing. The way you hold yourself, how you use your body. Stance: what you will see in all good dancers, actors, acrobats. The way a solo violinist stands before lifting his bow. The way someone in equilibrium enters a room. A combination of tension, pride, balance—standards.

(Standards...Ah, those things they still teach at the small conservatories of music and theater, starved for money...)

Style: without which we all slouch not toward Bethlehem, but toward the town dump, brothers and sisters to beer cans and the immortal shapes of plastic.

A FEW
HARSH
POLITICAL TRUTHS

The following is a transcript of a television interview on a touted talk show between a professional prober (PP) of the media, and myself.

PP: Before I ask any questions about your political beliefs, I would like to quote from something you've just written. It begins this way:

"This is the story," you wrote, "of a man who woke up one morning and found the dictionary changed. The word "freedom," for instance, was defined as "lack of control"; "liberty" as "freedom from responsibility," and "equality" as "the state of being no better than others." The definition for "progress" was "inertial guidance." But the thing that upset the man most was the definition of the word "liberal." It had the abbreviations for "archaic" and "obsolete" after it, and the comments: "formerly used to describe members of the Democratic, as opposed to the Republican, party in the United States, and to denote a belief in civil rights, social reform, collective bargaining, and international cooperation. It is also used in a general sense to imply futility, or loss of direction." Now my question: Are all liberals finished?

MM: As defined, they are obsolete.

PP: But you call yourself a liberal, don't you?

MM: I don't call myself anything. Other people do.

PP: You are a Democrat, aren't you?

MM: I am.

PP: But you say here, "there have been Democratic faces and Democratic evasions that turned the man's stomach, and even when a Democrat talked well, he said nothing new." If you really believed that, Miss Mannes, why are you a Democrat?

217

MM: I suppose because the Democratic past comes much nearer to what I believe than the Republican present.

PP: Then the Democrats have no future?

MM: Not until they make one for themselves.

PP: What do you consider a typical Republican?

MM: Someone with a strong sense of social status, however limited, and a deep allegiance to business, however big.

PP: Is there anything wrong with that?

MM: I'm not saying it's right or wrong. I could never be one.

PP: Why not?

MM: Because I don't believe in social status and I don't think that business is the primary aim of life. Republicans seem to me to be chiefly concerned with holding on to what they have, social position and respectability, or profit.

PP: You don't like respectability?

MM: I don't like people who are conscious of being the "right" people, and whether they are on top or not, Republicans have always considered themselves to be an elite of respectability. In business, being one is said to constitute a seal of integrity.

PP: Are you saying the Republicans haven't integrity?

MM: Let's pass over Watergate and much else. No party has a monopoly on integrity, or corruption. My point is that Republicans *think* they have a corner on morality, and Democrats don't.

PP: Are you saying that Republicans are snobs?

MM: Yes, but then, so are Democrats.

PP: What's the difference?

MM: In the nature of the snobbery. Democrats think they are more intelligent than Republicans. I prefer that to a social or economic basis of assumption, even if it is only an assumption.

PP: Are Republicans above the people?

MM: I'm not saying that. There is no question in my mind as to which party has concerned itself more closely with the needs of the people.

PP: Then why aren't the Democrats in power?

MM: People wanted a safe thing, and what they thought was a safe man.

PP: And didn't they get that?

MM: They got a vacuum.

PP: Which nature abhors?

MM: Which my nature certainly does.

PP: Do you mean to say that Republicans have no vision?

MM: I mean they have a restricted vision. They equate conservatism with caution, try to extend the known present into an unknown future with a minimum of change, and prefer conformity over diversity.

PP: Isn't this wisdom?

MM: I call it fear.

PP: Are you saying that Democrats have a monopoly on courage, vision, and intelligence?

MM: The philosophical and social premises of the Democratic party have more courage and vision than Republican party doctrines.

PP: Can you think of any circumstances in which you would vote for a Republican president?

MM: If a man like Lincoln were nominated. But that isn't possible.

PP: Because we no longer produce great men?

MM: No, because today, Lincoln would not be a Republican.

PP: Have your views affected your social or professional life?

MM: Socially, yes. My few Republican friends consider me unhousebroken. More expedient Democrats, including those who would jettison their party's heritage to win the White House again, are embarrassed by me.

PP: And professionally?

MM: An overwhelmingly Republican press is no help. But, there are more forums. After all, here I am—on the air.

PP: And here I am, off it. Thank you.

HANDBOOK
OF SUBVERSION

The following is a memo from the publisher of *The Daily Ruse and Smearer,* New York's greatest tabloid, to a new editorial writer.

Welcome aboard, Ed. I'm glad to have you with us, and I know our readers will be, too. You might regard this as a sort of primer of editorial writing, applicable to any situation or event or personality which you bring to public attention.

The most important thing of all is to know the people you are talking to and writing for: the millions of New Yorkers who buy our paper. Never overestimate them. They are not very intelligent, not very noble, and not very cultured. They are, in fact, semiliterate. They know very few words, so confine yourself to those words and don't use any of more than two syllables except for wholly familiar terms like "patriotism," "loyalty," "motherhood," etc. Above all, keep your sentences short. Our readers can retain only one thought at a time, so do not confuse them with several. The act of reading itself is difficult enough for *The Daily Ruse and Smearer* buyer: your job is to make it as easy as possible, as you would for a sixth-grader.

Our readers would rather feel than think. The emotions they like to feel most are hate, distrust, sexual desire, and vicarious violence. They also like to feel patriotic and victorious, but these emotions are secondary.

The sex and violence we handle adequately in our news items and photographs. Your job is to supply, regularly, objects for their hatred and distrust.

The most effective method for arousing hatred is to make them feel gypped, fooled, or betrayed.

Here are specific instances, which can be used repeatedly.
1. *Our so-called Allies.*
So-called is a useful phrase. The pitch goes like this: our

European allies are unreliable and ungrateful. We have spent x million for this and that (figures are always available), and what do they do for us? Our readers never fail to respond to the Sucker Sam and Money Down the Drain approaches. What they will not tolerate is any evidence to the contrary, which might dilute their anger.

2. *Liberals*

I.e., intellectuals, do-gooders, bleeding-hearts, fuzzy thinkers. There's still mileage in flogging this seemingly dead horse. The public has a taste for blood, and liberal blood tastes best. Lay off the scientists.

3. *The United Nations*

You can't ever miss on this one. Foreigners living off us and forced on us. Doubtful loyalties. Haven for spies. Nothing but talk. Play up an incident involving a delegate or employee, stressing alien ways, nuisance-value, taxpayers' burden, etc.

4. *Diplomats, ours and theirs*

The average American likes pot shots at diplomats (as above). Fancy-pants, la-di-da kind of thing, superior types who talk but don't act, live high, party where they please, etc. Here again we touch the core of *The Daily Ruse and Smearer's* philosophy: Action, of whatever nature, is superior to thought. Never mind buts and ifs, folderol and arguments. It's American to act. Hit hard and let the chips fall. Call a spade a spade, but don't insult blacks gratuitously. Give it to them straight, particularly the gays. Fancy talk is negotiation, and negotiation is concession. Americans don't concede or compromise. Remember *always* that the U.S. stands for moral values, other nations for self-interest.

5. *Socialism*

Push this one for all it's worth, all the time. Always equate socialism with Communism. Jump on anything that looks like it's going to hamper private interests.

8. *England*

There's a strong attachment to the British royal family, and we don't kick that around. But Americans always feel better when the

English look inferior. We've been galled since 1776 by the English assumption of superiority. Besides we don't like the accent. It sounds educated.

7. *Corruption*

Anger and resentment are easily aroused by suggestions of this, at the federal, state, or municipal level. These are pleasurable emotions for most people because by focusing guilt on others, they remain superior in virtue. Everybody likes to see somebody else get caught for the vices practiced by themselves. In spite of the fact that most of our readers are Democrats, there is an advantage to exposing Democrats rather than Republican corruption because then you catch the liberals, do-gooders, intellectuals, etc., on the same hook. Remember that Democratic corruption has a sinister core of purpose. Republican corruption is usually just plain stupidity.

8. *No-nos*

Because *The Ruse* is so easy to read and appeals to the simplest human instincts, a large proportion of its readers are in the following categories: the Irish, second-generation minorities like the Italian, German, Czech, etc., the American Legion and other patriotic groups (geriatrics, but vocally powerful), labor and white-collar workers; high school (as against college) graduates. Because of its innate conservatism and unswerving battle against Communism, *The Ruse* appeals strongly to Catholics also. It should be obvious that our uncompromising, hard-hitting honesty must not be expended on these groups. On the contrary, all unflattering references to any or all of these groups or persons must be omitted.

Never criticize the Irish, the Catholics (especially the Pope), the Jews, the police force, or bus drivers. Be careful with subway workers. Take issue, on occasion, with Protestants; they include liberals and they aren't well organized. Pick on individuals instead of groups.

Ed, that's all for now. Happy hunting, sharp writing, and kick 'em in the teeth.

Yours,

Al

CHICKEN

Does the world think Americans
are afraid of nuclear war and death? The
true Americans are not — Adv.

I'm not a true American,
I fear a nuclear war,
I fear the death of all of us,
I fear the fearless more:

I fear the true Americans
Who do not fear a war,
Who have not taught themselves to know
What human life is for.

I'm not a true American,
I'd rather live to see
The most exasperating peace
Than simply not to Be.

ONE GRAND JOUST ON THE
BARRICADES
(A SPEECH)
NOVEMBER 29, 1974

Before the night is over (don't worry, I talk short), I had better explain why I am often referred to in text and on air as "a cultural reactionary" or an "intellectual fascist." I like both of these, since my critics are exactly the people whose wings I like to pluck, and whose reactions prove my point.

The Point — and there will be more than one — is that a giant lipstick replanted at Yale is called Art; that a bundle of pipes arranged in a chaos of wire is sculpture; that graffiti on walls and subways are really a form of art — the cry of the desperate and oppressed; or that a canvas eight by ten feet, entirely white with possibly one wavering line at extreme left is, well, a painting. The best one can say of it is that it sure is minimal — along with the mind that made it.

To sum up, I can no longer stomach the results of an inflated ego deflating craft (man, what's that? who this broad think she is, the old M.F.?). I trust you know what M.F. means, it's just that I won't foul the Smithsonian air with the only language younger generations speak, y'know, like I said.

All this leads to the hyphenated word that for the last decade has raised all the above nonsense to something called "Self-Expression." Express yourself, and *Bingo* — you're a playwright, an artist, a painter, and a graffiti expert! The crucial question is never raised: What if the Self is not worth expressing? S-H-I-T, man, *no way*. Use a spray can, use cow dung, use crayons on monuments, use anything you can find in the back of a garage — set it up and it's ART — because you've *expressed* yourself. Wow!

I must here explain the violence of my disdain and often disgust at the violation of five thousand or more years of creation and craft.

Craft is the key word now, and I was lucky enough to be born of
parents who spent their life practicing the art that sustained not only
their public career but their private spirit...

I speak of music. From the age of three I would hear them—in
the living room, with curtains drawn across the double-door—
practicing at the violin and piano not only for the support of their
family but for a passionate love of the sonatas of Brahms and
Beethoven and Mozart and so many other great composers. When
they both felt a phrase was somehow not right, they would repeat it
until it was. And I—once standing outside the curtains listening—
was so upset when I heard them arguing that I cried. Once they
heard *me,* and immediately came to me—a child of five. They asked
me why I was crying, and I said, "Because you are not going to be
together anymore...you'll *leave* us!"

They comforted me with hugs and kisses and assured me that
these were only the little quarrels that most people had from time to
time...Look at the way my brother Leopold and I fought? Over tiny
things. And you still loved each other, they said.

I nodded, sniveling—and in time they resumed their practice
and I went and hung on my trapeze—I was an artist on my
trapeze—I could even hang by my feet!

I had also very demanding teachers at my French lycée on the
west side, one block away. The English teacher scared everybody—
sloppiness was for her a cardinal offense.

I will remember one scene till I die. Most of the class was about
fourteen or fifteen years old, and one girl we called Floppy had long
mustard curls hanging around her rather equine face.

Anyway, we were asked to get up, one by one, and tell what we
thought Keats's *Ode on Death* really meant.

When Floppy rose, she said "I know what it means, but I can't
express it."

Whereupon the diminutive Miss Sweet rose from behind her
desk and said: "If you *know it,* you can *express* it! That is precisely the
art of writing: to learn words so well, to understand them so well,

that they become the arts of thought and expression." (She did not say *self*-expression.)

She wasn't more lenient to me, though she encouraged me mightily. One day after class she beckoned me to her.

"I am very interested in what you write and how you think, but must you *always* fall in love with those heroes you write about?"

I lowered my eyes, terrified. She went on: "You know, it's either Sir Gawain of the Round Table, or Lancelot, or Danton, or Lincoln—or Mark Twain.... Why must they all be dead people?"

"Because"—I faltered, feeling tears—"because there aren't any like that alive!"

Briskly Miss Sweet said, "Now, now, stop taking everything so seriously. I just thought you might be a little more objective. Especially if you're going to tell the world the truth?"

She was right, by gum. I was already dreaming of myself speaking to multitudes of people of things nobody else had the courage to say. Anyhow, I played the martyr, sure that they would burn me on a pyre. (Sometimes they have.)

Regardless, from the great musicians who came to play at our house, from my brother's experiments in the long creation of color photography (Kodachrome) and from kind literary elders, I learned what craft meant. That if you didn't love something enough— whether it was a sunset or a deer or the faces of people or scudding clouds or your own inner depths—if you could not express these without mastering your craft, life was no good.

Experiments, yes. Approximations, yes. And all hail to amateurs in all fields who make things for love and give them to us as personal statements which cannot be called art, simply because craft is lacking. It's fun and games (and here I will give myself the luxury to say that the pioneer of all the sleazy abominations described as forms of art is Andy Warhol, who most certainly does not dwell in peace. He has done more than his share in elevating to stardom the garbage pail...along with an evil capacity to con a supine public.)

Honest experiments, yes. Times change, and so does man.

Experiments are fine if people don't have to pay for them in theaters or movies or galleries. Or look at them.

It's probably no wonder then that I could no longer endure seeing a huge steel construction crane — painted bright orange and labeled as art — towering over glorious patterns of trees in Central Park. I am just as annoyed by ponderous metal lumps or cubes shaped like giant molars, and planted bluntly before the usual white tombstones called architecture. Perhaps they deserve each other.

Possibly a kind word can be said for them in that they are not *even* self-expression — and so devilishly devised that you can't even sit on them. Give me Lincoln, anytime, sitting on his bronze chair. (Give *us* Lincoln anytime.) He wouldn't want to be so, but he sits as a constant reproach to the Union he saved, only to see it come apart . . . and to the hurrying little men with briefcases who pass him daily.)

But to come back to Self-Expression — and, briefly, to me. All I've been saying so far is a defense of craft and discipline as part of the artist's passion and dimension. I started by saying what my parents brought to this, but neglected to say that when they took my brother and me to Europe for their summer concerts in various countries, they also took time out to see the marvelous works of art — from Rome to Florence, from Venice to Milan — from Munich to London. My mother was a real Baedeker-hound, and there were moments when my father yearned for nothing more than sitting in a café outdoors and sipping a vermouth, and we young yearned for the side streets and back alleys, or a park and food.

But mother was right, because what we absorbed from Michelangelo's *David,* to Fra Angelico's paintings, from the Giotto frescoes to the ancient palaces; from Donatello's heads to the *Winged Victory* in the Louvre — all this never left us. For what it gave us was not only the purity of the making, but the passion of the feeling. These men — yes, they were all men! — were not expressing themselves. They were expressing the enormous hunger of their people for beauty, for a communality of feeling that enveloped the spirit while it nourished the eye.

We—my brother and I—never lost this feeling, and that must be why I miss it so desperately now in a culture absorbed in self and in administering shock treatments to an already numbed society.

Of course there are serious and highly talented artists now—and don't ask for a list because I can never remember all of them in a public place and at short notice. The same goes for composers. And all I will say about my intrinsic passion for music does *not* include much after Stravinsky, some Prokofiev, Satie, and a few others.

But not for the doodlers (what would be the tonal synonym for graffiti?). Certain popular current composers (who sound like a swarm of bees bugging a Moog synthesizer) have no more to do with the function and purpose of music than the orange crane with art)... well, let those fragmented souls who love it listen to it.

As for me, I still believe that America's greatest lyric gift of all is found in the scores of musicals. Gershwin, Cole Porter, Dick Rodgers, Lerner and Loewe—now *they* are among the kings of melody and rhythm and joy and sometimes tears that raise people above themselves and nourish their spirits.

Popular entertainment? Certainly. But so, in the past, were the embellishments of public art: the fountains, the churches, the squares, the touring actors and dancers. Out of their disciplines—and they were hard—came joy and humor and escape from reality.

So too, is the best of today's ballet. And no one here tonight needs to be told what the merciless training of a dancer is. Nobody without a deep inner passion for the art could withstand the effort. And only when a dancer survives this effort can a man or woman add that particular difference which infiltrates and inspires the real artist in any art: the difference that in turn—and finally—frees the dancer to express—within tightly limited lines—himself—and herself.

Perhaps the greatest current atrocity of quote self-expression—unquote—is the current use (heck, *abuse*)—of language...from high government and business down to the jargon of professions and of college seniors. "Like, man, y'know, so this dude comes along, y'know. ..." I will spare you more, partly because it is nauseating and partly because I have to express myself bountifully on this subject to the Council of English Teachers of America. (Y'know, man, those M-F S-H-I-T-S.) (I have been trained by television not to offend family viewers.)

If my point isn't clear by now, my self-expression urges me to shut up except for any questions you care to hurl at me.

Anyway, now you know what a cultural reactionary is, I fully expect some of you to hit me with lucite boxes, marble molars, or a concrete hexagon beautified by graffiti.

But this little old lady in sneakers can take it as well as dish it out. She'll just throw them back to you, and feel sorry for the people who made them and the critics who laud them.

Is there a bodyguard in the house? Must I express myself further?

NO!

THANKS!

ON MACHISMO

It's no wonder that a proposed law to ban handguns gets nowhere in our country. Under the guise of self-protection, any American can buy the weapon not only for his presumed defense but as a mark of his manliness.

The revolver is the metal twin of his penis. The difference is that the one can give death, the other life. The metal can maim and kill, the hardened flesh give pleasure and renewal.

This is not say that lover and gun toter are the same; only that many men need a projecting instrument to prove their manhood; or, if you will, their power, their dominance — whether in love or hate.

There are, of course, many men who prefer to aim their natural weapon and penetrate flesh and expel their power for love (or conquest) rather than hate.

But the twins of aggression and pride are shared alike by lover and killer. Inevitably the macho man must prove his power over women, subduing her to exalt himself.

This is why the macho man feels no more guilt beating his wife than flailing an enemy. The fruits of machismo then lie in suborning a real or imagined threat, and the cries of the stricken woman flutter and tear the flags of his conquest.

Perversely enough, the macho man, "conqueror" of women, suborner of their rights, betrays his weakness more than his strength. He must use force to prove his superiority, whereas the superior man needs only gentleness. The penetration of woman is then not an aggression but a coupling, in which he entrusts his natural weapon to its natural sheath.

For a woman who has never been beaten and is not by nature masochistic, it is hard to imagine the pleasure derived by some of our sex through force and violence. One can only infer that their image of themselves is so reduced, so prideless, that only attack and pain can prove their worth and masculine dominance.

Judging from the increasing instances (or perhaps, reporting) of battered wives, it would seem that far more women attract this kind of male treatment than we had heretofore imagined. Or, inversely, that men without outlet in war find beating women the easiest and most agreeable release for their gnawing aggressive instincts.

Of course, men need not physically abuse women to reduce their stature. In the corporate world it is far easier (if less exciting) merely to pull the ladder of ascent out from under them. To "put them in their place," so to speak.

Even easier is to reduce their sense of self-worth in the home. This men can do in multiple ways, from highly praising the dinner a married friend cooked for them the night before, to suggesting that their wife wore too much makeup.

Or they can sigh, with barely concealed annoyance, that their mate never read the book which everybody else was discussing.

Worse, for most women, is to see their spouses peering down the cleavage of a billowing female when their own breasts had hardly developed from the pubic stage, or were hanging listlessly to their laps.

This is worsened later in the privacy of their home by such husbandly remarks as "Why don't you try one of those snappy bras—you know, the ones that cross over and push up?"

This can only be followed by a nastily snappy comeback like "Why don't you cross over and push up!"

Unfortunately most women cry inwardly, eaten by envy and cursed by fate.

Of this their mate is sublimely oblivious, resigned through long years to yearnings for what his wife may lack, and at moments venting his loss on her, in various ways.

Whatever the form of diminution of women: battering or diminishment or rape, it is the weak man who must use it. That this weakness can range from the street bum and the animal adolescent to a corporation official is merely consistent with the fear-contagion in almost all men: that they are not strong enough, or, at least, not as strong as they should be.

ON LOOKING
YOUR AGE

There is no trick in being young: it happens to you. The process of maturing is an art to be learned. By the age of fifty you have made yourself what you are, and if it is good, it is better than your youth. If it is bad, it is not because you are older, but because you have not grown. Yet this is obscured, daily, hourly, by the selling of youth. Look young, be young, stay young. And with this mandate, millions of goods are sold and millions of hours are spent in pursuit of a youth which not longer exists and which cannot be recaptured.

The result of this effort is, in women, obscene; in men, pathetic. For the American woman of middle age thinks of youth only in terms of appearance, and the American man of middle age thinks of youth only in terms of virility.

The streets of American cities are full of thin, massaged, madeup, supported, tinted, overdressed women with faces that are repellent masks of frustration; hard, empty, avid. Although their ankles are slender and their feet perched on backless high-heeled slippers, they fool only themselves. The obscenity in all this is that our advertising media has conned these women into using outward techniques of sexual allure to maintain their youth when they are no longer desired by men.

By the time a woman is fifty, she is either wanted as a woman of fifty or not really wanted at all. She does not have to fool her husband or her lover, and she knows that competition with women far younger than she is not only degrading but futile.

When I see old people in villages in France or Italy, I am struck by the age of all women who are no longer young, and, at the same time, startled by the beauty of their old faces. Lined and grooved and puckered as they may be, their hair grizzled or lank, they make their glossy contemporaries at a bridge table here seem parodies of women. They show that they have lived and have not yet found the means to hide it.

I never thought of my mother in terms of age. Whatever it was at any time, she looked it. Nobody then told her to lose weight or do something about her hair because she was far too interesting a human being to need such ameliorations. I don't doubt that, given today's aids, she could have looked younger and smarter than she did. But she would have lost something: her identity.

At club gatherings, hotels, and resorts, the older women of America look identical. What lives they have led have been erased from their faces along with the more obvious marks of age. Their lotions have done well. But I wonder if all self-deceptions do not harm, and if their price is not loss of self.

I wonder, too, if the intemperate natures of many younger women today might be caused by this same hard finish, this self-absorption, of older women to whom they might otherwise turn. I cannot imagine going for counsel and comfort to a mother or aunt or grandmother waxed, tinted, and masked to look my age.

The fight is not for what is gone but for what is coming, and for that battle, fortification of the spirit is paramount, the preservation of the flesh a trivial second.

Let the queen bee keep her royal jelly. Or so I keep telling myself.

WAKE UP
AND READ

*Air Force scientists have been
teaching octopuses to "read."*

Down on the sea bed, a book in every arm
See the giant cephalopods in literacy's charm;
Publishers are jubilant, for now at least they know
Each volume will sell eight-fold (or squid pro quo).

MY
RESURRECTION
(FROM *THEY*)

I love the sea: it is my resurrection and my life, the fluid in which I was born, the element which sustains. I give myself to it. It lifts and pummels and threatens and caresses, it makes me whole. I am in awe of its ferocity, grateful for its calm, amused by its perversity.

To be inland is a deprivation, as if, as a child, to be kept from a mother.

I am awed by a handful of sand, by the knowledge that each grain is a rock, a crystal, a boulder, a carapace. I enlarge them in my mind.

The shapes of shells catch my breath, even fragments indicate perfection. The sight of porpoises leaping is a leap of joy. The inside curl of a wave is miraculous.

So are the small birds pecking at the shoreline and the tern in a vertical dive and a wedge of duck winging so fast, and the stretched black necks of cormorants.

An ocean and beach in fog may be mystery but it has the stillness of truth. You wait, and the truth has to come.

THE LUCKIEST
PEOPLE
(FROM *THEY*)

I drink to the artists: those who make beauty, who unlock mysteries, who serve truth.

Artists never make wars. They are too busy making life out of the matter of their visions. Only artists are timeless. They may abhor death as the arbitrary end of their search, but they need not fear it, for what they have done of real worth lives *for* them.

We are no better people than others, but we have had better lives than most. We are the luckiest ones on earth.

So many in this world are starved while we are full. So many feel impotence while we are vested with power. So many are bound while we are free. Between the poles of arrogance and humility, between failure and triumph, we walk alone, listening to voices unheard by others.

But *our* voices are heard. And in the measures by which we love what we do, we are loved by others.

You have called me prejudiced. I am. I am prejudiced against the stupid, the brutal, the lying. I am prejudiced against those who destroy and those who appease them.

But I am for the few anywhere whose gifts set them apart as guides and leaders, who are by talent and wisdom and integrity superior. I am for the aristocratic tradition, without which no civilization can exist.

So I drink to my civilized — my immortal — friends!

ET TU, BRUTE

Arteriosclerois in Animals and Birds is up Tenfold—"Social Pressure" Cited.

If the bellbird is bats and the gnu is
gnurotic,
If the crocodile's crocked in his pool,
If the buffalo's bushed and the pseal is
psychotic
And the potto's beginning to pule,

It's the faces, the faces, from morning
till night,
The faces outside of the cage,
It's the terrible faces forever in sight
That accelerate animal age;

That wrinkle the wrhino and cripple
the crow
And tire the testy toucan,
For there's nothing that wears out an
animal so
As the bestial stare of a man.

HOW DO
YOU KNOW
IT'S GOOD?

Suppose there were no critics to tell us how to react to a picture, a play, or a new composition of music. Suppose we wandered innocently into an art exhibition of unsigned paintings. By what standards, by what values would we decide whether they were good or bad, talented or untalented, successes or failures? How can we ever know that what we think is right?

In criticism or appreciation of the arts, it has become fashionable to deny the existence of any valid criteria, and to make the words "good" or "bad" irrelevant, immaterial, and inapplicable. There is no such thing, we are told, as a set of standards. This has been a popular approach, for it relieves the critic of the responsibility of judgment and the public of the necessity of knowledge. It pleases those resentful of disciplines; it flatters the empty-minded by calling them open-minded; it comforts the confused. Under the banner of democracy and the kind of equality that our founding fathers did *not* mean, it says, in effect, "Who are you to tell us what is good or bad?" This is the same cry used so long and so effectively by the producers of mass media who insist that it is the public, not they, who decides what it wants to hear and see, and that for a critic to say that *this* program is bad and *this* program is good is purely a reflection of personal taste. As Dr. Frank Stanton, a former president of CBS Television, commented at a hearing before the Federal Communications Commission, "One man's mediocrity is another man's good program."

There is no better way of saying "No values are absolute." Another aspect to this philosophy of laissez faire is the fear, in all observers of all forms of art, of guessing wrong. This fear is well come by, for who has not heard of the contemporary outcries against artists who later were called great? Every age has its arbiters who do not grow with their times, who cannot tell evolution from revolution or the difference between frivolous faddism, amateurish experimentation, and profound and necessary change. Who wants to be caught *flagrante delicto* with an error of judgment as serious as this? It is far safer, and certainly easier, to look at a picture or a play or a poem and to say, "This is hard to understand but it may be good," or simply to welcome it as a new form. The word "new" in the U.S. has magical connotations. What is new must be good; what is old is probably bad. And if a critic can describe the new in language that nobody can understand, he's safer still. If he has mastered the art of saying nothing with exquisite complexity, nobody can quote him later as saying anything.

But all these, I maintain, are forms of abdication from the responsibility of judgment. In creating, the artist commits himself; in appreciating, you have a commitment of your own. For after all, it is the audience which makes the arts. A climate of appreciation is essential to its flowering, and the higher the expectations of the public, the better the performance of the artist. conversely, only a public ill-served by its critics could have accepted as art and as literature so much that has been neither. If anything goes, everything goes; and at the bottom of the junkpile lie the discarded standards, too.

What are these standards? How do you get them? How do you know that they're the right ones? How can you make a clear pattern out of so many intangibles, including that greatest one, the very private I?

For one thing, it's fairly obvious that the more you read and see and hear, the more equipped you'll be to practice that art of association which is the basis of all understanding and judgment. The more you live and the more you look, the more aware you are of a consistent pattern, as universal as the stars, as the tides, as breathing, as night and day, that underlies everything. I would call this pattern and this rhythm an order. Not order, *an* order. Within it lies an incredibly diversity of forms. Outside of it is chaos. I would further call this order, this diversity held within one pattern, health. And I would call chaos, the wild cells of destruction, sickness. In the end, it is up to you to distinguish between the diversity that is health and the chaos that is sickness, and you can't do this without a process of association that can link a bar of Mozart with the corner of a Vermeer painting, or a Stravinsky score with a Picasso abstraction; or that can relate an aggressive act with a Franz Kline painting and a fit of coughing with a John Cage composition.

There is no accident in the fact that certain expressions of art live for all time and that others die with the moment. Although you may not always define the reasons, you can ask the questions. What does an artist say that is timeless; how does he say it? How much is fashion, how much is merely reflection? Why is baroque right for one age and too effulgent for another? Why is Sir Walter Scott so hard to read now, and Jane Austen not?

Can a standard of craftsmanship apply to art of all ages, or does each have its own, and different, definitions? You may have been aware, inadvertently, that craftsmanship has become a dirty word because, again, it implies standards, something done well or done badly. The result of this convenient avoidance is a plenitude of actors who can't project their voices, singers who can't phrase their songs, poets who can't communicate, and writers who have no vocabulary, not to speak of painters who can't draw. The dogma now is that craftsmanship gets in the way of expression. You can do it better if you don't know *how* you do it, let alone *what* you're doing.

I think it is time you helped reverse this trend by trying to rediscover craft: the command of the chosen instrument, whether it is a brush, a word, or a voice. When you begin to detect the difference between freedom and sloppiness, between serious experimentation and egotherapy, between skill and slickness, between strength and violence, you are on your way to separating the sheep from the goats, a form of segregation denied us for quite a while. All you need to restore it is a small bundle of standards and a Geiger counter that detects fraud.

In time, you will acquire an instinct born of experience and association that will allow you to separate intent from accident, design from experimentation, and pretense from conviction. You may have to go partway or even halfway to meet the artist, but if you must go the whole way, it's his fault. Hold fast to that. Somewhere along the line you can learn to distinguish between a true creative act and a false arbitrary gesture, between fresh observation and stale cliché.

Purpose and craftsmanship, end and means, these are the keys to your judgment in all the arts. What is this painter trying to say when he slashes a broad band of black across a white canvas and lets the edges dribble down? Is it a statement of violence? Is it a self-portrait? If it is *one* of these things, has he made you believe it? Or is this a gesture of the ego or a form of therapy? If it shocks you, what does it shock you into?

And what of this tight little painting of bright flowers in a vase? Is the painter saying anything new about flowers? Has it any life, any meaning, beyond its statement? Is there any pleasure in its forms or texture? The question, inexorably, is whether it is good. This is a decision which only you can make for yourself. It takes independence and courage. It involves, moreover, the risk of wrong decision and the humility, after the passage of time, of recognizing it as such. Entrenched prejudices, obdurate opinions are as sterile as no opinions at all.

Yet standards there are, timeless as the universe itself. When you have committed yourself to them, you have acquired a passport to an elusive but immutable realm of truth. Keep it with you in the forests of bewilderment. And never be afraid to speak up.

REQUIESCAT
IN ORBITUM

*Space "burial" problems are probed
by Aerojet-General scientists. They con-
clude the best solution on a multi-crewed
deep space mission would be a "space
version of burial at sea." A dead astronaut
"should be simply pushed into space
where his body would vanish into the
vastness."*

Push me simply into
space
And leave me on my
way
Running an immortal
race
With night and day.

Then I would be free at
last,
A particle of air,
Worm and fire
bypassed
And coffin bare.

Whiter than a sailor's
bone
Washed in the deep,
I with my starry own
Would vigil keep.

A LIVING
WILL

In one year, over fifty thousand Americans wrote to the Euthanasia Fund in New York for free copies of "A Living Will." Requests are multiplying steadily. The "will" is a shortened testament addressed to a patient's family, physician, clergyman, and lawyer. It says in part, "If there is no reasonable expectation of my recovery from physical or mental disability, I request that I be allowed to die and not be kept alive by artificial means or heroic measures."

"I do not fear death," the document continues, "as much as I fear the indignity of deterioration, dependence, and hopeless pain. I ask that drugs be mercifully administered to me for terminal suffering even if they hasten the moment of death."

The Living Will has no legal weight, but the addressees can seldom ignore it with conscience.

Death in the right circumstances is both right and our right. If we have lived to the fullest of our capacities, dying is merely suspension within a mystery. If our lives have seemed wasted or futile, death is more reprieve than reprimand.

Believing this, we should not be intimidated or thwarted by the counterarguments of the state, the Church, the law, society, or medicine itself. We have heard them all, but the final choice must be ours.

This is why I now express my own terms in the matter of life and death. It is meant to be neither a model nor an example. Yet if it gives direction and courage, it will have served its purpose.

To: My Doctor - _____(name)_____

My Lawyer - _____

My Closest Relative - _____

My Dear Friend - _____

I ask each of you, in concert or individually, to assure that certain measures be taken to end my life should I fall victim to the following circumstances. Singly or together, they would deprive me of all that I cherish most in living, and prefer death to that loss.*

1. Any disease or accident that would leave me unable to take care of my own bodily functions or deprive me of independent mobility.

2. Progressive deterioration of mind as evinced by total loss of memory, only partial consciousness, chronically irrational behavior, delirium, or any other evidence of advanced senility.

3. Any condition requiring the use, beyond two weeks, of mechanical equipment for breathing, heart action, feeding, dialysis, or brain function without a prognosis of full recovery of my vital organs.

4. Any progressive deterioration of muscle, bone, or tissue requiring an increasing dependence on intravenous substances, and without realistic hope, for recovery consistent with my definition of such.

5. I do not wish to survive a stroke that impairs my ability to speak or move, nor any accident or disease resulting in vision too impaired to see or read, or in total deafness.

A world without beauty heard or seen is no world for me.

A life without freedom and movement is no life for me.

If age and illness deny me these, I choose death. And if a difference of opinion among you results in ignoring or only partially acceding to these requests, then I beg that one of you provide me with the means to take my own life while in a conscious state.

---

*Note: This document to be re-signed by me every two years up to and until the event that loss of consciousness through accident or illness precludes my signature. In this case, the wishes expressed are to be carried out by the person herein addressed.

ON GOD
AND DEATH:
THREE VIEWPOINTS

If I were asked if I believe in God, I would say that I do not know. I believe in a grand universal order and meaning, and in a power that is both greater than us and within us. But I do not believe in the God worshiped formally in churches, a God that answers prayers, that guides and shapes, that comforts and chides, that is, when you really come down to it, a benevolent and all-seeing entity built recognizably in man's image. I certainly do not believe in the God that is invoked by our public characters as an ally in righteousness. He would be a shabby God indeed.

But I do believe in a great many things that formal worshipers of God profess to believe, and they are not abstracts but the highest purposes for which man exists. To believe, with passion, in justice, in kindness, in decency, in humility, in courage, and in honor, it is not necessary to believe in God. It is necessary only to be aware of the magnificence of the universe and the wonder of man himself, both part of a cosmic pattern revealed equally in a raindrop and the chorales of Johann Sebastian Bach.

What can a minister give me that Beethoven cannot? What can a church give me that a Piero della Francesca cannot? What can a sermon give me that I cannot find in a Shakespeare sonnet or the lines of great philosophers and poets? What can church ritual give me that great dance cannot? All these creative acts lift, shrive, and enlarge man, balancing humility with a prodigious urge towards light. Pettiness falls away, supplanted by compassion. Who, seeing and hearing these things, can bear to destroy?

So, too, can the shape of a leaf or the palpitating body of a bird or the swell of a cumulus cloud be of infinite succor. What can be found in a church that is greater than these things?

Only, I think, the words of Christ. And I, for one, would far rather read them in solitude than hear them intoned and explained in company. I doubt if any greater disservice has been done to Christ than the manner in which his teachings are presented in a thousand pulpits across America: self-righteously, mournfully, nasally, coldly, feebly, flamboyantly, blandly, violently. If you have forgotten what it can be like in church, turn on your radio some Sunday and hear how a man can desecrate Christ.

There are ministers who give the Gospel its full beauty and power, and many thousands of people who derive guidance and comfort from listening to them, attesting to a deep need for spiritual formality in a society so lacking in social form. Massed worshipers appear to need, too, a sense of communion with others in sharing beliefs. They cannot arrive at a single vision by themselves; others must define and support their truth.

"Not all of me shall die'," whispered Shulubin, another patient in Solzhenitsyn's *Cancer Ward*, quoting Pushkin. "Not all of me shall die."

> Kostoglotov groped for the man's hot hand lying on the blanket. He pressed it tightly. "Aleksei Filippovich," he said, "you're going to live! Hang on, Aleksei Filippovich!"
>
> "There's a fragment, isn't there?...Just a tiny fragment," he kept whispering.
>
> It was then it struck Oleg that Shulubin was not delirious, that he'd recognized him and was reminding him of their last conversation before the operation. He had said, "Sometimes I feel quite distinctly that what is inside me is not all of me. There's something else, sublime, quite indestructible, some tiny fragment of the universal spirit, Don't you feel that?"

Great creators have not only felt this, but through the relentless passion of their talents, expressed it in testaments that have defied time and death.

One of the wisest comments on the phenomenon of the creator and death is the passage by J. W. N. Sullivan, the musicologist, in a book on Beethoven, published in 1927.

Beethoven's late music communicates experiences that very few people can normally possess. . . .They correspond to a spiritual synthesis which the race has not achieved but which, we may suppose, it is on the way to achieving.

Beethoven's great predecessor, Mozart, wrote to his father, Leopold, in 1787.

Since death (properly understood) is the true ultimate purpose of our life, I have for several years past made myself acquainted with this truest and best friend of mankind so that he has for me not only nothing terrifying anymore but much that is tranquilizing and consoling.

Jump less than two centuries and hear what Albert Einstein wrote to the family of his lifelong friend, Besso, who died exactly thirty-four days before Einstein himself succumbed: ". . . Now he's gone slightly ahead of me again, leaving this strange world. That doesn't mean anything. For us believing physicists, this separation between past, present, and future has the value of mere illusion, however tenacious."

At a time when astronomers report that stars and quasars are "waltzing in space," who can doubt him? The "tiny fragment" that no one can define still defies extinction. It is also the product of human consciousness and choice.

Eternity will be
Velocity or pause,
Precisely as the candidate
Preliminary was.

                                                        — Emily Dickinson

A novel of mine written in 1947 was drawn from the diary of a woman who had died and who retained her consciousness of earth only when those she knew and loved were thinking of her. The flyleaf of this novel, *Message from a Stranger*, quoted Joseph Conrad: "the dead can live only with the exact intensity and quality of life imparted to them."

Here is the heroine's description of her death:

"Then it happened. I remember one final spasm, not unlike the birth of Philip. And I remember thinking to myself, this must be the delivery of my soul; and then I saw a primitive Italian painting in reds and blues where, from the prostrated body of a noble lord, escapes the white puff of his spirit, freed. But there was a strange addition: I was for a time both the bearer and the borne, the issuant and the issue. I was at the same moment creating and being created, and I could not tell which was the more arduous: the black, hot fighting up into light, or the more familiar expulsion of my burden...

First with a fearful roar and clanging, as if a thousand metal hearts were beating against their walls, I was whirled into an emptiness as crowded with a substance as are certain silences with sound. It was a wild and headlong flight, when I spun and reeled... like a leaf in a hurricane. In all this roaring...there was music, phrases, voices, instruments engaged in some gigantic, cosmic tuning up; a perpetual prelude—to what symphony...?

"The headlong rush...then stopped, and a great silence came. I seemed to be quivering like a seismographic needle; suspended in a stationary dance as a part of some microscopic palpitation. This dance took place in an electric and impalpable space that had no boundaries.

I was not alone. In this featureless state there was a definite pattern, of which I was only one point of many. I remember once seeing a "model" of an atom, several white balls jiggling around a central ball. This, presumably, was the final breakdown of matter.

A great peace settled over me. I had not realized until this moment how heavy was the burden of identity.   (1978)

I know now that the burden of lost identity, as in the trapped and helpless and dying, is even worse.   (1985)

Index of
Names

249